D0755492

Lillian Too's
Book of Gold

Lillian Too's
Book of Gold

Wise Ways to Health, Wealth and Happiness:
365 Daily Reflections to Enrich Your Life

RIDER

LONDON · SYDNEY · AUCKLAND · JOHANNESBURG

First published in 2001 by Rider, an imprint of Ebury Press, Random House, 20 Vauxhall Bridge Road, London SW1V 2SA www.randomhouse.co.uk

Random House Australia (Pty) Limited 20 Alfred Street, Milsons Point, Sydney, New South Wales 2061, Australia

Random House New Zealand Limited 18 Poland Road, Glenfield, Auckland 10, New Zealand

Random House South Africa (Pty) Limited Endulini, 5A Jubilee Road, Parktown 2193, South Africa

The Random House Group Limited Reg. No. 954009

Papers used by Rider are natural, recyclable products made from wood grown in sustainable forests.

Typeset by SX Composing DTP, Rayleigh, Essex Printed and bound in Italy by Graphicom Srl

A CIP catalogue record for this book is available from the British Library

ISBN 0-7126-0214-3

C O N T E N T S

F O R E W O R D

This book reflects on different manifestations of the inner self.

The inner self glows with soothing wisdom and healing light bringing realisations that have the ability to comfort you, enrich you, empower you and alleviate your ills. The inner self condenses experiential insights that contain all one needs to live a fuller, richer, more empowered life.

Developing inner insights bring us the wisdom to live from moment to moment. Begin with the premise that your life is precious, that it is one continuing dynamic – changing, evolving and transforming from moment to moment. Your life, and your perception of all that it comprises, reflects the attitudes of your inner self. Knowing this, you will start to live in a state of awareness. It is then that wisdom realisations begin to surface and all your high moments become more intense and all your low moments more bearable.

The reflections in this book contain the seeds for inner wisdom to emerge.

Let these reflections open your mind to an understanding of happiness and an appreciation of abundance, of feeling enriched and empowered, of being confident and strong. Let them open pathways, allowing you to view inner and outer insights in the light of a greater perspective. These insights are powerfully experiential!

Wisdom and understanding unfolds as you relax the mind, enabling it to flow freely within your consciousness. It is then that the higher realisations of the spirit begin to unfold. Concepts of karma, of change, of impermanence, and the precious quality of life take on new meanings that have the potential to comfort, empower, and open your eyes to the fabulous value of your inner instincts. Let your mind lead the way.

JANUARY 1

WITH YOUR VERY FIRST BREATH THIS YEAR ...

Visualise the gold that lies within your heart. The gold within you is far more precious than the gold in your wallet or your bank account. Watch your breath, and let it awaken you to the rich and abundant world within you. Your breath should be neither too deep nor too shallow. Just breathe steadily and calmly as you lift your heart and take your first tentative steps into a whole new world. A world of inner abundance – of health, wealth and happiness which, when found, instantly illuminates and enriches your life.

JANUARY 2

PAUSE AND REFLECT ...

What does your life mean to you? Why be sad when you can be happy? Why feel poor when you can feel rich? Why hesitate and hold back when you can move forward and on? Why feel bad when you can feel good? Flow with life itself. Just follow the words of wisdom contained in this book and let me share an alternative perspective with you.

JANUARY 3

JUST THINK HOW LUCKY YOU ARE ...

You are fortunate simply to be alive, to be able to make choices and to live the kind of life you wish. Your karma is incomparably excellent. If you start from the premise that you have good luck, you will attract even more of it! It is the mind that brings health, wealth and happiness. It is the mind that leads you to discover all the secrets of the world, secrets such as discovering the real path to genuine and permanent happiness.

JANUARY 4

YOUR BREATH IS MAGICAL ...

Delight in it. Your breath has the power to warm freezing hands, yet when blown onto a bowl of hot soup it cools the soup. Good fortune comes when you harness the environmental breath that surrounds you. It is similar to your human breath, but infinitely more powerful. It is known as the Dragon's cosmic breath, or chi. Chi is the invisible inner energy that adds luminance to your life.

JANUARY 5

TUNE INTO YOUR INVISIBLE CHANNELS ...

When you exercise your body and give it some fresh air, you are energising the breath or chi inside you. This is why you always feel good after a brisk run. When you run, you are encouraging the wind channels inside you to open. So as you run, tune into the invisible channels within you. Visualise fresh, transparent chi as white light flowing into your body down through your head into the three vertical channels of your body, purifying you mentally and bringing about a lightness of being that is instantly refreshing. Try this the next time you feel low. Get some yang energy inside you to beat the blues!

JANUARY 6

FEEL THE GROWTH ENERGY OF A TINY SEED ...

Imagine a tiny seed sprouting in the spring and becoming a beautiful new plant. Your life is like the seed. With care it can burst into full bloom. The seed benefits from the growth energy of the wood element. Place lush plants in the East and Southeast corners of your home to energise the symbolic wood element and then think of growth energy filling you. You must truly want to grow. If you do, your reflections themselves become powerful laser-like energy centres that will fill you with sufficient chi to develop, expand and become enriched!

JANUARY 7

TRIM THE TREE TO LET IN THE SUNSHINE ...

Feng shui is primarily concerned with balance. It's a harmonious blend of yin and yang, neither too little nor too much. All of life and living requires this balance. A tree that grows wild and is never pruned is like a life with no direction. Trees bring health and well being when they create both yin and yang. When sunshine is blocked, yin dominates and your life goes into a tailspin. Your health, in particular, could suffer. But when trees get trimmed regularly, they send out new shoots, soak in the summer sun and even burst into bloom. So trim that tree!

JANUARY 8

DRESS UP YOUR ROOM WITH FLOWERS ...

Fresh flowers symbolise precious life energy. They mask unsightly, harmful edges and create yang energy. Flowers revamp a faded room instantly. If you need cheering up, put some beautiful, fresh flowers in your home; they will make you feel happier straight away. Just make sure you change them the moment they start to fade because fading flowers suggest an ending, emit harmful chi, and look ugly. Even the water that nourished them has become stale. Remove them immediately. If you do not want to use fresh flowers, artificial flowers are to be preferred over dried flowers.

JANUARY 9

FEEL THE VITAL LIFE FORCE OF YOUR PET ...

Pets are such good life energy to have around you. They remind you there are other realms of existence and make you realise how lucky you are to have been born human. Pets also enhance the feng shui of your living space especially if your home is left unoccupied and silent through the day. Pets symbolise the vital life force bringing yang energy into a house made yin by the silence of being unoccupied. Be kind to your pets. Remember karma and feel compassion for them having been born into the animal realm of rebirth. In their realm they are unable to develop the kind of inner spirituality that you are able to. Reflect on how marvellously lucky you are to just be you!

JANUARY 10

BIRDS ARE LIKE THE PHOENIX ...

Birds also represent natural, vibrant, animate life energy. They are very yang and it is especially happy yang! Birds belong to the Phoenix family and these winged creatures bring opportunities that have the potential of ripening into great success. So feed the birds around your home, make friends with them and invite them into your world. If they trust you sufficiently to nest within your garden they will bring you great good fortune that particularly benefits your children. Speak to them of life and love, and share your inner hopes and aspirations with them. Let these winged creatures take your wishes into the cosmos, imbuing them with a special energy. Who knows then when they might just surprise you with some totally unexpected miracle!

JANUARY 11

SEEING YANG THROUGH YIN ...

Weeding your garden presents a great opportunity to meditate!
When you weed your lawn imagine that you are throwing out
what you don't need. As you tread carefully in between the blades
of grass, feel that you are clearing the clutter of your outer living
spaces. As you work, allow the free flow of thought. Let your
mind take you where it will. Who knows, if you concentrate on
each individual blade of unwanted grass long enough you might
well be like Einstein who discovered his famous formula while
looking at the sunlight filtering through a blade of grass. See yang
through yin. Encourage the emergence of brilliance.

JANUARY 12

SUMMARISE YOUR ANGER ...

How stunningly relieving it is to sit down and summarise all the wrongs that you feel have been done to you. Review everything that incenses you; the unfairness of this world; the stupidity of your boss; the annoying habits of your colleagues. List everything down. Replay all those moments when you lost your temper. Watch as your mind grows angry again and again. Everyone should do this exercise once a week until there are no more afflictions left to catalogue. You will soon discover there are numerous less boring things to do with your time than to fuel your anger!

JANUARY **13**

BURN YOUR NEGATIVITY ...

A very effective method I use to shake off feelings of anger, hurt, worry or despondency is simply to burn them. I write down everything that bothers or upsets me and then either tear up the list, flush it down the toilet or burn it. I have discovered that burning is the most effective. As I burn the piece of paper I visualise everything that upsets me vanishing into thin air like smoke, and like magic it really does happen that way!

JANUARY 14

MIST IS BEAUTIFUL BUT FOG CAN BE DEADLY...

Have you ever considered the way you look at things? Next time you look at clouds let your inner mind trace images that project some secret story from within you. Do not worry if your initial steps of self-discovery are small steps. Every journey has to have a beginning. Seeds give rise to gigantic trees. First steps lead to fantastic journeys. This is the year that you will discover the gold inside you. The only prerequisite is that you must want to discover it. You must want to find before you can find.

JANUARY 15

LIKE FINDING TREASURE ...

When you are inspired by some great purpose, some extraordinary project, all thoughts break their bonds. Your mind transcends limitations, your consciousness expands in every direction and you find yourself in a new, great, and wonderful world. Dormant forces, faculties and talents suddenly become alive and you discover yourself to be a greater person than you ever dreamed yourself to be. It's like finding treasure! Like finding gold!

JANUARY 16

THE GOLDEN GLITTER OF YOUR INNER MIND...

Your inner mind has great power to enhance your life. It shines like the sun and flows in an avalanche of abundance. When you welcome this glow, all your needs, desires and wants are met instantaneously, for you will always be one with your inner self, and the inner self is everything. You will discover that all you will ever require is already within you. So tune inwards. Remove the stains of outer negatives. As you polish away layers of grime and dirt the lustre within is uncovered and the glow of inner gold is revealed. Inside you there is a veritable storehouse of great good luck just waiting to be released. This is how luck works.

JANUARY 17
THROW OUT YOUR WORRYING ...

Today, try throwing out all your worries. Worrying only gets in your way. It keeps you from being you; it prevents you from performing, from discovering the wonderful treasures within you. The Dalai Lama once said, 'Why worry if you can do something about your problem. And why worry if you cannot?'

JANUARY 18

PICKING UP THIS SPECIAL THING ...

When you find it, this special thing, pick it up! Don't let it go! Place it at your front door so you feel its essence each time you step in and out of your home. Nothing will ever get you down again. And what is this special thing? It's called Non-attachment. Develop the ability to stay detached from things, people and outcomes. Make the effort to do this! Nothing makes for a calmer and more aware life than embracing this wonderful practice of non-attachment.

JANUARY 19

A LITTLE HOUSE CLEANING ...

Do some house cleaning today! Throw away some of your old things. When you let go of things you will start to feel the energy of your space getting lighter, brighter, whiter. Let your cleaner surroundings lift your spirit and make you feel good. Spring-cleaning makes your inner abundance closer within reach. When you finish cleaning and clearing, take some incense sticks and walk around each room allowing the incense to purify your outer space. Chant a favourite mantra as you walk slowly round the rooms of your home and imagine the chi of your space getting lighter and brighter.

JANUARY 20

LET THE MORNING SKIES ENTERTAIN YOU ...

If you have never done this, take an early morning walk. Do this at least once in your life. Watch the setting of the moon and the rising of the sun. There is nothing more magical and inspiring than watching a silent, silver moon fading alongside the flaming yellow rising sun. You will feel your spirits lift as you watch the magnificent grandeur of moon and sun. Then suddenly, with a burst of yang energy, you will feel the impossible become possible.

JANUARY 21
DRINK SOME HERBAL TEA TODAY ...

Learn to differentiate between green teas and dark teas, between light teas and heavy teas. Buy yourself a tiny set of terracotta teapot and tea cups if you want to drink the dark, heavy teas. These teas should be allowed to brew for a few seconds only and then drunk in a single gulp. The Chinese believe that drinking tea is a worthwhile companion to silent reflection. Tea allows the mind to grow calm and the body to wind down. And as you relax your inner tranquillity takes you to the Pure Land of the Immortals.

JANUARY 22

TUNE IN TO YOUR LEVEL OF PATIENCE...

Today, ask yourself, how stoic is your attitude towards things that inconvenience and upset you? How far would someone have to push you before you retaliate, before you break your cool and allow the dam of suppressed annoyance to overflow? We each have our own tolerance level and when you know yours you can then begin to work at raising it. Dealing with circumstances and people that test your forbearance is a wonderful way of pushing aside many of the causes of unhappiness. The moment you touch base and arrive at a level where nothing, absolutely nothing, causes you even the slightest shred of annoyance you will have found the way to permanent happiness. Think about this.

23
JANUARY

ARE YOU A RABBIT OR A WOLF?

Do you hop around, run, and burrow deep into the earth when confronted with obstacles and danger, feeling safer in the familiar terrain of your own home, or are you a wolf who hunts far and wide, playing the role of the aggressor? When you go deep within yourself would you be brave enough to venture forth or would you find comfort in the safety of the familiar? Think about it! Are you a seemingly timid person whose life philosophy is to avoid trouble or are you a predator whose very stance inspires fear? Are you happy being what you are or do you harbour a secret desire to change?

JANUARY 24

IF THREE PEOPLE WERE HOSTILE TO YOU TODAY...

Go and look at yourself in the mirror. Maybe you're frowning too much. Maybe you're sending out unfriendly signals. Think how much nicer the world would be if you just consciously smiled a little more. A smile will soften all the furrows of your brow. It will make you feel better as you become aware of your mouth muscles relaxing. Do it right now. Give yourself a secret smile and feel your mind experience happiness immediately.

25

JANUARY

ARE YOU ARE A DRAGON OR A TIGER – YIN OR YANG?

Dragons and tigers are the celestial creatures that reflect the yin and yang of the cosmic man. When you are very aggressive and brave, you are said to be most yang, like the courageous celestial dragon soaring ever upwards. When you are protective and attack only when provoked you are said to be most yin, like the ferocious giant pussycat they call the tiger. Stop and think! Are you a dragon or a tiger personality?

JANUARY 26

GET A FOOT MASSAGE...

Massaging the extremities of the body – the hands and the feet – gently dissolves blocks in your inner systems. Find someone to rub the undersides of your feet and press away the aches and pains of the physical body. This will clear the obstacles that impede the flow of chi within you. Foot reflexology balances the inner systems, and with your blood and life forces flowing unimpeded inside you, the chi within you will move unhindered. This is one sure way of enabling the radiance of the gold within to transcend the body and shine forth. You will simply glow with good health.

JANUARY 27

ARE YOU RULED BY YOUR HEART OR YOUR HEAD?

Such a clear-cut divide separates the emotional types from the logical, or so it seems. The truth of the matter is our hearts and our heads rule us all in varying degrees and it really does not matter which holds the greater sway. These are all merely labels and categorisations that mean only what you want them to mean. Don't let yourself get stereotyped. Instead watch yourself and note those moments when the head reigns supreme and other times when the heart simply must have its way.

JANUARY 28

REJOICE IN SOMEONE ELSE'S TRIUMPH...

The greatest joy is to be able to feel really good about someone else's triumph. To rejoice in another person's moment of glory, and more, to be gracious enough to feel genuine admiration at an opponent's magnificent and honourable victory will make you feel good. It is the ultimate rejoicing because it manifests a generous heart at a spiritual dimension. Let feeling good about your loved ones' triumphs be good practice for extending this generosity of spirit to others. And then you will know the real happiness of selfless rejoicing.

JANUARY 29

WHAT KIND OF GODDESS ARE YOU?

Are you a mother Goddess who nurtures, a Seductress Goddess whose beauty enslaves, or a Goddess who personifies sensuality? Women play many roles in their journey through life. Feel free to take on the role of the Goddess of your age. But listen to your inner wisdom when it tells you it is time to transform from one God or Goddess to the next. When you listen to your own insights you will feel the joy of transcendental fulfilment.

JANUARY 30

RADIATE A SILENT POWER...

Tap into unseen forces within you. Reach inside for the wisdom, the strength and the power of silence. It is there – your inner force. Think of it as a bright, white light inside you. Feel it move along the pathways of your body. Feel it light up your heart, your throat, and your head, and soon you begin to exude an effortless strength that speaks volumes. Feel this strength today. Feel the strength of body, speech and mind.

JANUARY 31

ARE YOU A SCHOLAR OR A WARRIOR?

Which would you rather be? The scholar's pen is mighty, but is it more or less potent than the warrior's mighty sword? The more civilised the society in which you live the more powerful becomes the written and spoken word while the less civilised your society is, the more powerful becomes the sword or the bullet. The ideal is for you to be the warrior whose wisdom arises through scholarship; your mind is your key weapon rather than sheer strength or physical prowess.

FEBRUARY

ARE YOU A BASE CHAKRA PERSON?

Satisfaction comes from assuaging the needs of all the seven chakras in your body. But it is all right to take your time. Remember to satisfy your base chakras first before attempting to energise your upper chakras. Unless your belly is full it is hard to think of spirituality. And unless you have satisfied all your baser instincts you will constantly yearn for them. What I am saying is that as long as you are still a base chakra person fuelled by material goals, you cannot think of your upper chakras. So stay cool. Your time for spiritual awakening has not come yet, but it will! It is perfectly fine to move up your chakras at your own pace.

FEBRUARY 2

DARE YOU TUNE INTO YOUR UPPER CHAKRAS?

From the heart to the throat to the forehead and finally the crown – as you move upwards along your chakra points to finally reach your upper chakras, you are opening energy centres that take you deeper and deeper into your own spirituality. Who knows what waits within the inner core of you? If you wish to try unlocking these chakras simply close your eyes, and visualise bright white light at these chakra points. Stay relaxed and grounded while doing this and sit in a meditative posture. Activate your upper chakras only when you are ready.

3

DO YOU BELIEVE BLACK CATS BRING GOOD LUCK?

Do you believe that seeing a lame dog foretells of some misfortune or that dreaming of tigers indicates the second coming of a new spirituality in your life? Beliefs are never intrinsically true or false. Everything is a mirror of your mind. If it makes you feel better to believe then do so. And if it hurts you to believe, then don't. The key to happiness is to stay in control of your mind. Choose then to believe in things that bring you happy thoughts. If you have a black cat believe that this brings you luck and it will!

FEBRUARY 4

WOULD YOU WALK UNDER LADDERS?

I would not. Why should I tempt bad luck to descend on me? What does it cost me not to walk under a ladder? Nothing. So why should I walk under one? If I do it to prove a point, it is only my ego that is motivating me and since my ego is an illusion I would not walk under a ladder. My attitude towards superstitions has always been one of relaxed respect. Beliefs for me are real when I believe in them. I trust my instinct and so if someone else does not believe what I believe, it's cool. To each their own. It's your choice to believe or disbelieve. If a superstition costs you nothing much where's the harm in believing? And if it costs you dearly, where's the harm in not believing?

FEBRUARY 5

HAVE YOU CHECKED YOUR ELEMENT?

The Chinese believe everything in the Universe is composed of water, wood, fire, earth or metal. This principle of the five elements holds the key to unlocking the secrets of heaven, earth and man. When you know your self-element it identifies the nature of chi within you and then you will know how to enhance your chi. You will also know if the special person you just met will be good for you and whether the direction in which you are lying is bringing you luck while you sleep. It's a good idea to check your element. It could make your life flow seemingly smoothly and effortlessly.

FEBRUARY 6

DO YOU BELIEVE IN MAGIC?

Magic is simply the manifestation of objects, events and occurrences that we don't understand. A couple of hundred years ago the iron birds that fly through the skies would have been considered magic. Fifty years ago satellite television would be magic and just twenty years ago mobile phones would be magic. The more we believe in magic the more it manifests before our eyes.

FEBRUARY 7

ARE YOU A LEFT OR RIGHT BRAIN PERSON?

They say our left brain makes us logical and deductive, and our right brain makes us sentimental and creative. The truth of the matter is that we all have both left and right brains. So we all have the potential to be frightfully logical and also gloriously emotional. How could one possibly exist without the other? Our brains are thus an ultimate manifestation of the cosmic principle of yin and yang, opposites that contain a kernel of the other.

FEBRUARY 8

WHICH OF THE SEVEN PLANETS APPEAL TO YOU MOST?

Each of the seven planets – Sun, Moon, Venus, Jupiter, Saturn, Mars and Mercury – stands for many different things in different cultures. The coincidence is that they feature in almost all traditions and lineages of the metaphysical sciences. So if you seem to have a natural affinity to any one of the planets – it reflects something important inside you that is worth checking out. These seven planets reflect your seven chakras, stand for different colours and numbers and different high notes on the musical scale. Planets tell us a great deal about ourselves. Knowing your ruling planet could tell you more about yourself. Reflect on this for a moment.

FEBRUARY 9

DO YOU KNOW YOUR FACE TYPE?

Did you know that men with square faces tend generally to do better in life, rising more easily to positions of eminence? Such men are more successful than men whose faces sport other shapes. And did you also know that women with oval shaped faces are the ideal, indicating the kind of life that brings ease and luxury with little effort? Look into the mirror and check out your face type. If your face shape is less than ideal you can always resort to make-up!

CAN YOU SEE A TRIDENT ON YOUR LEFT PALM?

A trident is like a fork and if it occurs in any one of the mounts on your inner palm, it is said to bring great good fortune. A trident coming out of your vertical fate line brings enormous career success, while a trident at the top of your vertical sun line indicates success with lots of money. So check to see if you have this trident. If you cannot detect a trident in your palm look for a fish sign. This too, is a sign of wealth!

HAVE YOU CHECKED THE SOLES OF YOUR FEET?

Look for birthmarks on your feet that reveal something special about you. Did you know that if you have a small black dot – or a mole on the sole of your foot, it indicates that at some stage in your life you will be recognised as a special person? Black or red spots anywhere near the feet also indicate plenty of travelling luck. The more hidden they are the more luck is indicated. I have been interested in the signs of the physical body ever since I learned about the marks and signs of Buddha, the Enlightened one, so next time you see a spot on your body it could mean something significant. It could take you on a labyrinthine journey that leads you to a pot of gold underneath the rainbow. All you need on this voyage of discovery is to be courageous.

12

HOW MANY NATURAL BRACELETS DO YOU WEAR?

Turn your hand around until you are looking at the insides of your palms. Now look and see how many lines there are at the base of your palm. The lines should be firm and unbroken. Two lines on both hands indicate moderate luck. Three lines on the working hand bring luck in the professions. Three lines on both hands bring wealth luck. Check now and see if you have the potential to become wealthy. Spiritually rich people tend to have three of these natural bracelets.

13

THE LENGTH OF THE FINGERS INDICATES MATRIARCHAL POWER.

In both men and women, when the middle finger is longer than the index and ring fingers it indicates that they have the upper hand in the home. When the ring finger is longer than the index finger a woman will be more successful than her spouse. When women have longer index fingers and rigid thumbs they tend to be very dogmatic!

FEBRUARY 14

BRUSH YOUR SCALP AND MEDITATE ...

Invest in the best hairbrush you can find. Allow your thoughts to drift along unknown pathways as you brush. Think of energy gently flowing inside you, overcoming bumps, blocks and obstacles. Then think of your life flowing smoothly along like this. One hundred strokes of the brush each evening is all you need to take stock of where you are at, in any moment in time.

FEBRUARY 15

PRETEND YOU ARE THE BEST...

When it comes to attracting good fortune in your career believe
you are the best in your field. Pretend, if you have to. When you
develop this attitude your inner consciousness will manifest
abilities within you that you never knew existed. Remember that
you are a fertile ground of many untapped talents! Do this with the
humility that expects to be surprised.

FEBRUARY 16

FEELING GOOD...

The secret to health, wealth and happiness is simply to work at feeling good every single day of your life. Feeling good comes from the serenity of being on top of things. It comes to those who can feel that their life is solid, has a purpose, and is secure and meaningful. Feeling good comes from feeling confident. It is an inner conviction that you possess the answers you need for understanding, coping and overcoming any tough day that comes your way. Tap into your powerful inner strength for it knows where to find answers, and where to seek solace and comfort.

FEBRUARY 17

LIFE IS AN ODYSSEY OF FRESH INSIGHTS...

Try looking at an old routine in a new way today. Or look at someone you see every day in a new way. Do this consciously. Let something that you do daily reveal a fresh new insight for you to take joy from. Let it be a new way of looking at a daily predicament, like working out the best route to get to work. Or creating a brand new attitude towards an office colleague you hardly noticed before. Feeling good is to know you can remould your reactions in accordance with each new circumstance, and each new way of viewing things. Then life becomes a continuing odyssey of fresh insights and sometimes quite exciting discoveries. The person you took for granted and previously dismissed could well turn out to be a soul mate. Just being prepared to look at anything, or anyone in a different way can usually generate some pleasant surprises.

FEBRUARY **18**

MAINTAINING BALANCE...

Hostile scenarios often come as surprises. Do not let intrigues, politicking, problems, or betrayals that force their way suddenly into your existence faze you for longer than an instant. Obstacles to feeling good usually cause a momentary imbalance that can give way to panic reactions that can be unsettling. This can lead to a sudden flow of negative emotion and destructive energy, which manifest in anger and temper. If this happens, focus immediately on maintaining balance. Internal balance instantly soothes strong reactions. Consciously take a very deep breath, making it especially slow on the out breath. Another technique is to do the opposite of what you are doing when you go out of sync. So if you are sitting down, stand up. If you are standing, take a seat. Make yourself smile if you are scowling, and smooth the lines on a furrowed brow.

FEBRUARY 19

THERE ARE NO FIXED RULES...

There can be no fixed rules to feeling good. There is no end to the permutations of life's circumstance, the variations, twists and turns are exactly the things that make up the substance of one's life. Every new day is then an adventure into the infinite. Viewed this way it is easy to continuously profit from every new experience gained in the course of living.

FEBRUARY 20

EACH DAY BRINGS NEW REALISATIONS...

Each new day brings new sensations and new feelings. Simply being prepared to paint new experiences and realisations with a positive glow is all that is required to move happily from one day to the next and from each year to the next. The contemplations and musings in this book of days are prescriptive as well as reflective. Some are known truths that simply remind, while others represent a new way of looking at issues that may require a transformation of attitude on your part. Go with the flow.

CYCLES OF NATURE HAVE A DEEP PURPOSE...

We seem to be constantly reminded how quickly time passes. Already we are in another new year, a new millennium. Soon, it seems, the snows will melt once more and we will be looking forward to Spring. I know that in the forests the animals presently in deep hibernation will soon burrow their way from underground to greet the new season. They have slept through the deep cold of winter and will soon emerge a year older. Even the trees seem to be waiting for the sliver of sunlight that will bring the warmth that will enable them to burst into bloom. It seems to me cycles in nature have a deep purpose.

FEBRUARY 22

THE PRECIOUSNESS OF HUMAN LIFE...

The cycle of the seasons reminds me of the constant and continuing change around us. These cycles tell us how vulnerable we all are to the passage of time. They make us see how deeply precious time really is. The only certainty in our lives is that eventually we must die. And the only thing in the world that is uncertain is the time of death. You may be alive today yet in an instant your life can get snuffed out, so you should not waste your time on earth. Your life truly is much too precious to waste.

BETTER TO BEND GRACE-FULLY THAN TO STAND INFLEXIBLE...

The other day I saw a tall, majestic looking tree uprooted and humbled by the unexpected severity of a storm. It was a sad sight. It made me think how the very strength and pride of the tree had made it inflexible and thus vulnerable to the fierce wind and rain. All around the base of the tree tiny blades of grass able to bend with the changing winds survived the stormy weather. How sad that the humble and lowly grass seems so much better equipped to survive the howling winds and rainstorms. Better, it seems, than the stronger and mightier tree. Like the grass perhaps we too should bend gracefully rather than stand inflexible in the face of difficult and adverse circumstances.

FEBRUARY 24

THINKING OF SUNNY DAYS...

You can make yourself happy simply by thinking of sunny days. Coming out of winter the sun seems especially embracing. And even in countries that get bright sunshine all year round people never tire of the joy of sunshine. On days when you are feeling especially low for no reason at all, you are probably missing the vital yang energy of the sun. If this is so, the next time there is bright sunshine take a hand-held crystal outside into your garden and hold it directly up to the sun. It takes only a moment for the crystal to absorb the heat that captures the energy of the sun. Then wrap the crystal in silk.

CREATING BEAUTIFUL
APPEARANCES...

At the heart of feeling good is looking good. Making yourself look good is an excellent way of making yourself feel great. Beauty is as enticing as a sweet smelling body, so lay it on! Try soaking in a bath of scented water filled with seven types of flowers. These signify the lovely attributes of the seven planets – the Sun, the Moon, Jupiter, Venus, Mars, Saturn and Mercury – then massage in some aromatic oils before slipping into the most beautiful or expensive outfit you have. The ritual of looking and smelling good will take at least an hour and by then whatever was ailing you will have dissipated in the glow of your freshly pampered body. When you make yourself look good, you will feel wonderful. This is a happiness ritual that never fails.

FEBRUARY 26

HAPPINESS IS WRITTEN IN YOUR STARS!

Here's a little secret. Your happiness is written in the stars – your astrological stars. As long as you are convinced of it, it is so. I always believe all the good things my fortune-tellers tell me. The secret is to forget everything negative, bad or unlucky. In my scheme of things there is no such thing as a future of inauspicious luck. Over the years I have also succeeded in developing a selective memory, which convinces me I was born lucky, born special and made for happiness. It is the same with the events of my life. I make a point to record only events that make me happy. Photographs that make me feel unattractive are instantly torn up and thrown away, never stuck in photo albums to strike a chord of unhappy times. This way I never relive them. So the smart thing to do is to consciously paint happiness stars in your astrological chart. Over time these will be the only stars there!

FEBRUARY 27

A PICTURE IS WORTH A THOUSAND WORDS...

Images convey powerful moods and nuances. They provide the backdrop against which the mind digests the messages conveyed by the words inside your head. So when you want to reach deep within yourself to tap the power that lies inside you, think about images. You can bring yourself into a frame of mind, which will dissipate all negative feelings simply by holding an image of a smiling you clearly in your mind. Make the effort to recall a happy moment that caused you to break into a wide, wide smile. Your mood will improve the very instant you visualise a happy you. Imagining a happier time will immediately cause all unhappy thoughts and negative feelings to dissipate and fade away. Such is the awesome power of your very own smiling face.

FEBRUARY 28

YOU CAN BE A GENUIS IF YOU WANT TO BE...

Being a genius is well within the scope of every individual. If you want to be a genius begin thinking with your conscious mind, and simultaneously feel with your subconscious mind. Make an effort to combine intellect with intuition. Think with your head but also go with the intuitive mind that will take you to places within your self that you have never been before. But I have a better proposition. Forget about being a genius. Seek instead to awaken all the amazing abilities that lie dormant within you. There is incredible ability and strength inside us we do not know we have. Let me explain. The power is inside you, and it starts with the mind. As long as the mind can visualise your ability to do something, your inner power will actualise it for you. The only thing required is a strong and unwavering belief in yourself. This is what sets all the creative energies in the universe into motion to make your visions into reality.

FEBRUARY 29

EAT WELL AND BE STRONG...

This is such a fundamental rule of living yet so many people systematically hurt their bodies, their minds and their spirits by not eating well. It seems as if the whole world is on some diet or other. If you want to be happy, feel good, feel strong and feel energised make sure you eat well. Did you know that hunger pangs, arising from skipping meals, could make you ill-tempered and depressed? So eat well today. Get yourself a good book on nutrition and understand your body. When your body is well your spirit feels good. When your body is unwell, your spirits sag.

MARCH

A GOOD MORAL CAUSE MAKES VICTORY VERY SWEET...

Since forever, certainly for as long as I can remember, good has always triumphed over evil. There seems to be an inexhaustible energy source in the universe, which releases an abundance of energy to bring ultimate victory to the moral high cause. This is because deep in the hearts of men lies goodness. This seems to be the very essence of humanity. So when you are championing a good cause, and you are laying yourself on the line and feel afraid, just think how wonderful this all is to the human spirit. A good moral cause makes life and all your victories very sweet indeed.

MARCH 2

WHEN YOU WIN, BE MAGNANIMOUS...

There is every reason to be generous when you are the victor and nothing at all to be said in favour of playing the all-conquering winner who merely burns and destroys. It is those people who leave the vanquished with nothing who simply cannot enjoy their victory. These are the people who will one day feel the bitterness of total defeat. Even when it is your most hated enemy that you have vanquished, do not deprive yourself of the sheer joy of feeling magnanimous. Nothing tastes sweeter than the victory that enables you to languish in the self-created glory that comes with the manifestation of a genuinely big heart. Victory will be sweet for you will have the opportunity to be truly compassionate.

MARCH 3

SEASONS CAN SOMETIMES GET OUT OF SYNC...

Have you ever thought of what life would be like if winter dragged on and on with no let up? Just think if there really was no end in sight to the bitter January cold. How many creatures would freeze and starve to death? How many plans would go askew as you waited in vain for spring to arrive, and then suddenly the heat of the summer sun greeted you instead of the beauty of the glorious transitional season between winter and summer? And when summer is prolonged the earth gets parched and bodies get burned. Sometimes seasons do seem to get out of sync. We should learn our lessons from the regularity of seasons. In it we see the true essence of the natural wisdom of the cosmos. Like the seasons, we should bring order into our own lives.

MARCH 4

A SUDDEN RELEASE OF ENERGY BRINGS A MOMENT OF BLISS...

Did you know that immediately after a moment of intense activity there is usually stillness? This allows the mind and body to recoup and recover. Think of lightning. In the darkness of the night sky a sudden streak of lightning lights up an entire city sky. It is like the unleashing of destructive tension. That moment is also excruciatingly beautiful and awesome. And then what follows is the cleansing rain, which prepares the land for the peace and quiet that follows. So it is with the human psyche. When you experience a sudden release of energy, what follows is to be savoured.

MARCH 5

GOING WITH THE FLOW IS OFTEN EASIER...

Sometimes when you fail to realise an ambition, your higher self may be trying to tell you something. Your inner wisdom may be sending you a message that there might be something better, more fulfilling which can be yours, which you haven't yet considered.

The river of life is often a winding course. Sometimes when you travel down this river it appears to be flowing in the wrong direction or there may be tributaries, dead ends and other distracting views along the way. Rivers also hold hidden demons that can rear their ugly heads at every curve and turn. Relax and enjoy the ride. Go with the flow. It is an easier and more harmonious ride than trying to struggle against the currents.

MARCH 6

EARTHQUAKES LAST BUT FOR A MOMENT...

The one positive thing about natural disasters is that they are seldom prolonged. Usually they last only for moments. Such moments can cause a colossal loss of life and represent a terrible tragedy. Yet they do not go on and on. A volcano erupts and then stops. An earthquake shakes the earth and then stops. A hurricane sweeps across the land and then dissipates. Man-made disasters, like wars, however, simply go on and on and on. You can do your little bit for humanity. Do not start wars or conflicts with people. They never end. If you are arguing with someone right now, end it immediately.

MARCH 7

APPARENT COINCIDENCES OFFER DIVINATION INSIGHTS...

All of life's coincidences are in reality no coincidence at all. When you live in a state of conscious awareness it is not difficult to find linkages between every event and every circumstance that happens and every person who appears in your world at any moment in time. Looked at this way all of life's 'coincidences' offer divination insights. Think through the last few days, all the things you did, all the thoughts that crossed your mind and all the people who touched your existence. Then meditate on the things that link them all. You might begin to realise some insights you had earlier missed.

MARCH 8

VIEW EVERY OBSTACLE AS A RIPENING OF NEGATIVE KARMA...

If you view every obstacle, difficulty and failure you experience as a ripening of negative karma, you will find it easier not to be defeated by the doors that get slammed in your face. View every difficulty in your life as a purification of some kind, and rejoice in the knowledge that you can emerge from these manifestations of rejection a stronger, braver, and wiser person. This way you will find that moving forward becomes easier. With doors so firmly closed behind you the only way open to you is to move resolutely forward!

MARCH 9

ACCEPTING CHANGE, IN ANY FORM, MAKES COPING EASIER...

Change can creep up on you like a stealthy stranger in the night, or it can descend suddenly in a shower of midnight snow, transforming the scenery outside your bedroom window when you awake in the morning. Change can reveal itself in slow motion or drop at your feet with a loud thud! Change can be painful, but it need not be so. Look forward to change and accept whatever it brings, no matter what form it takes. Change is inevitable; acceptance of it makes change a lot easier to cope with.

MARCH 10

BONDAGE IS A MENTAL THING ...

Many people live their lives as if they were confined to a gilded cage, not realising the door is open and unlocked and that they can soar to heights beyond their own imagination. Instead they build walls around themselves, afraid of the unknown, scared to fail, tormented by fear, troubled by what they believe are their inadequacies. Bondage is a mental thing. Free your mind, and your spirit will be free, and then nothing can hold you back!

MARCH 11

RECALL ONE COURAGEOUS MOMENT OF YOUR LIFE...

Think of the last time you made a courageous decision and, in doing so, bring back the memory of that moment. Courage is a feel-good attitude, which has the substance to sustain you through all those moments in your life when you feel weak, inadequate and defeated.

MARCH 12

THE VIRTUE OF ABUNDANCE...

There is simply no virtue in being poor or destitute. Virtue lies in thinking of abundance. When yours is a life brimming with love, happiness and wealth – you can rejoice in your good fortune. You can rejoice that you have the resources to make many people's lives happier and better. Abundance is not about being rich. It is about being rich and generous, about being compassionate and genuinely wanting to share; knowing how to use your wealth to help others. Then, and only then, abundance becomes a virtue.

MARCH 13

LET THERE BE NO IMPATIENCE IN YOUR LIFE...

Savour each day as if it were your last. Do not rush to keep
schedules and meetings. Slow down! Take your time! Do
something each day to make life meaningful. Make someone happy
today. Ease another's suffering today. Share something of yourself
today. Spare some of your time, not just for a friend, but also for a
stranger. If you want to reduce your sense of rush and to feel
good today try doing just one of these things.

MARCH 14

THERE ARE NO FRIENDS AND NO ENEMIES...

There is a Buddhist tale, which speaks of mixed reincarnations, where best friends reincarnate as sworn enemies in a new lifetime and previous enemies are reborn as sons or daughters. There is a lesson in this and that is that in truth you should have no friends and no enemies in life. All things manifest from the mind. It is the mind that labels friends and enemies. It is far better to label everyone as fellow beings – neither friends nor enemies. If you think this way you can create an instant antidote for attachment and anger, two poisons that are the cause of much suffering and pain.

MARCH 15

TUNE INTO OTHERS AND YOU WILL SEE MIRACLES...

It is when you consciously tune out of yourself and tune instead in to others that your ears and eyes begin to adjust to seeing all the miracles that abound around you. Between sunrise and sunset, marvel at the blossoming of flowers, at the birth of a new-born baby, at the rain drops bringing water from heaven, at the crops growing in the fields, at how much you are loved, and how much you have to be thankful for.

MARCH 16

BECOMING AWARE OF THE PATTERN OF THE COSMOS...

There is no such thing as coincidence. Nothing occurs by chance. There is a pattern in the cosmos, a reason for every occurrence, a purpose in everyone's life and a part to play in the unfolding universe of life. Everything happens for a reason. But the reason may not always be what you expected! When this happens let your response be gentle and patient. In time you will see how the pattern is unfolding. Until then develop an acceptance that enables you to go with the flow and prepare for when the reasons become gloriously meaningful!

MARCH 17

WHEN YOU'RE ON A ROLL, ENJOY IT!

This happens when you are in perfect harmony with the cosmos, when everything goes right and the golden road ahead of you promises to be as smooth as silk. These are moments of triumph, of success and of victory. At such times smile, savour the moment and feel proud and good about yourself. Don't let anyone spoil such moments for you. They are too precious, for moments like these happen in everyone's life in order to nurture our spirits and to remind us of the nobility inside us.

MARCH 18

EMBRACE THE MYSTERIOUS...

There are many unsolved mysteries in this world, like the mystery of instinct, of psychic phenomena, or of energy patterns. The inexplicable should inspire you to reflect on the boundaries of your conventional world. Do not be afraid of what you do not understand. Embrace the unknown with an open mind. It has been the slow unfolding of the mysterious that has brought us to the edge of our world today. Don't reject being a part of any world.

MARCH 19

ALLOW YOUR IMAGINATION TO SOAR...

Today you should open doorways to fresh ideas. Think of Einstein resting on a summer's day, his eyes half closed, looking at the sun's rays through a blade of grass and allowing his mind to travel with the ray of light. Let your imagination take you to places you have never been. Creativity unlocks brave new worlds and feeds your senses. Don't deprive yourself of it!

BRAVERY IS WASTED WHEN MOTIVATED BY GETTING EVEN...

Suddenly, negative thoughts interfere with the sanity of our positive world. Having developed courage and strength and determination we suddenly feel an urge, a need to get even with someone, something, some institution. If you harbour such thoughts remember there should be a higher purpose to courage and determination, and to being positive. These lofty attributes are wasted if the driving force that impels us to act is motivated by any thought of revenge.

MARCH 21

BE LIKE THE WAXING MOON...

A waxing moon gains in brightness with each passing night. Hour by hour, the light grows brighter, fuller, more luminous. Think of the moon's bright light inside you. Feel the bright, white light growing stronger and deeper. Then feel it radiate outwards in luminescent, shimmering waves that make every living being the glow touches happy, safe and warm. If you do this visualisation every day over fifteen days as the new moon gradually develops into the full moon, something truly wonderful will awaken within you.

MARCH 22

IF YOU FEEL A NEED FOR SILENCE, THERE IS NO NEED TO EXPLAIN...

However short-lived, silence makes you tune within, and makes you cut out distractions. Silence can be a great antidote for all kinds of suffering and grief. If there is a time in your life when you feel a need for silence, retreat into yourself gracefully. There is no need to explain your silence to anyone.

MARCH 23

EVEN A BAD DAY HAS ITS DECISIVE MOMENT...

Be sensitive to that moment and transform the tide of negative feelings before they overwhelm you. Remember that every bad day has a precise moment when you stand at the brink of falling over defeated, or standing tall, unvanquished. That is the moment to be strong.

MARCH 24

FEEL THE QUIET STILLNESS WITHIN YOU...

There is often a tranquillity you will find within you, especially when the external environment is filled with thunder and lightning. Rainstorms are great moments to reflect on the pervasive silence within. When torrential rain pours down it is easy to release any tensions and allow the rain to purify your thinking.

MARCH 25

HUM A MELODIOUS TUNE...

Music will change the vibrations that surround you. Happy songs lift the spirits like nothing can! Control your moods with music. Make it happy music. In fact it is an excellent idea to make it a rule never to listen to melancholic music. And if you enjoy love songs go for those with a happy ending. Singing the blues is like chanting a negative mantra.

MARCH 26

FAITH IN ONESELF COMES WITH PRACTICE...

If you live your life with faith in yourself, soon it becomes solid as a rock, unshakeable, unbreakable. Faith comes with practice. When you believe in something wholeheartedly that belief rules your conscious and unconscious moods like nothing can. So it is worthwhile to make sure that the faith you develop is in yourself, and the motivation behind your faith is rooted in making yours a life that is honourable and meaningful.

MARCH 27

MEDITATION ALLOWS THE INNER HIGHER SELF TO EMERGE...

Meditation is an exercise in mental clarity. You can meditate while eating, sleeping, and walking. Each time you think seriously you are doing contemplative and analytical meditation. The more you meditate the easier it will be for your higher self, your clever self, and your wiser self to emerge. When you sometimes wonder where some sudden brilliant insight came from, you can be sure it came from your own higher self.

MARCH 28

YOUR HIGHER SELF HAS REAL POWER – USE IT!

There are many names you can use for the higher self. And many different methods you can use to delve deep within yourself to access this higher self. Relaxed meditative sessions often yield positive results. With practice you will come to realise the value of what lies within you. Your higher self is your inner wealth, your inner gold. It is wise beyond words and it is your most trustworthy ally. Its power lies in the awareness it creates within you and the clever insights it offers you to navigate through the labyrinth of your life.

MARCH 29

MANIFESTED FANTASIES MAY NOT BE WHAT YOU EXPECTED...

Every positive thing you have ever heard and read about the power of the mind, and especially the subconscious mind is true. All the fantasies you have ever had can indeed be manifested into splendid reality but manifested fantasies may not seem as desirable once they become real. You should be careful what you wish for. In the harsh light of reality fantasies can sometimes become nightmares!

MARCH 30

MEDITATION SHOULD HAVE A HIGHER PURPOSE...

My very revered high lama, who is wise in the ways of the yogic, once told me that meditation should have a higher purpose. It should achieve far more than merely to teach you relaxation and dissolve the pressures of daily life. Meditation can open up far more noble pathways to permanent happiness. 'How?' I asked. I was told that it was by meditating on the right kind of subjects, such as how precious our lives are, and how we can strive for permanent rather than temporary happiness.

MARCH 31

STRIVING FOR PERMANENT HAPPINESS...

Walking along the spiritual path under the guidance of a qualified teacher represents a search for permanent happiness. Your guru should be someone who holds a lamp that lights up the dark pathways of the night. Your teacher should lead you along, step by step, towards a goal that represents not simply liberation from endless cycles of suffering lives but also to the ultimate realisation of the true nature of existence. Your spiritual guide will bring you to sudden enlightenment, a state of permanent happiness where sorrow has simply ceased to exist.

APRIL

WHEN YOU ARE READY THE TEACHER COMES...

It is true that when you are ready, when you have reached a certain point in your spiritual journey, the teacher will materialise in to your world. How this happens I really cannot tell you, but a true guru will appear in your life when you are ready. Mine did. He came into my life without warning and in a form I hardly expected. But his presence in my life has transformed my whole existence, my attitude, my mind and my reason for living. Suddenly for me, fulfilment has taken on real meaning. It will be the same for you. When you are ready the teacher will manifest in your life taking on an identity that will be the most beneficial for you.

APRIL 2

EVERYTHING UNFOLDS IN TRUE PERFECTION...

When you believe that you are truly part of the cosmos, when you sense the unfolding feeling of complete freedom that comes with accepting a new consciousness, everything will happen perfectly for you. You will feel yourself growing and expanding in new directions. You will get the conviction that anything can happen at any moment for you. Every dimension of you will grow and flourish.

APRIL 3

YOU CREATE YOUR OWN REALITY...

The truth of the matter is of course that you create your own reality. You possess the power that drives you onward and forward. The teacher guides you along, gives you the tools to unlock your own potential, teaches you, but you are the consciousness and the life force, the engine, if you like! It is you who holds the key to your own power.

APRIL 4

MENTAL SPRING-CLEANING...

If any cobwebs still remain inside your mind, which obscure your vision of your true nature, you must sweep them away! Your mind is like a mirror. When it is clear images reflected are sharp and lucid. When the mind has delusions, negativities, inhibitions and complexes accumulated over a lifetime what gets reflected is blurred, unfocused and misleading. So it is good to undertake mental spring-cleaning regularly. Sweep away the dirt that clouds your visions!

APRIL 5

EXCESSIVE PRESSURE CONFOUNDS DESIRED OUTCOMES...

Everything has a right and a wrong time to appear. The mind has to rid itself of excessive attachment to a desired outcome and be at peace with itself. When that happens, the prized result materialises more easily because it is no longer hampered; the pressure created by the mental attachment no longer exists. When you understand this, your cherished expectations will begin to take on greater success potential.

APRIL 6

BURNING ALL DELUSIONS...

Delusions are another word for the negative attitudes that hold so many of us captive. So many people never realise that when they feel insulted the slights are merely mirrors of their own minds. Delusions cause pain and suffering because they make you sensitive to imagined abuse, insults or loss of face. Today, sit down and burn all your delusions. Simply refuse to feel slighted or insulted again. That is the key to real happiness in all the relationships in your life.

APRIL 7

TROUBLED SPOTS THAT CREATE BLOCKAGES...

It is the troubled spots in your mind that create blockages to
success, happiness and well-being. The Chinese are great believers
in never allowing anything to obstruct the flow of chi, the life force,
within their mind, their body and their space. And with good
reason too. Blocks cause real problems. Get rid of them before
they become permanent.

APRIL 8

TRY EATING HUMBLE PIE...

When things look rough and problems mount, don't let pride make matters worse. Try eating humble pie and change your mental attitude towards the things that are going wrong in your life. Sometimes just looking at things from another perspective will provide you with all the right answers.

APRIL 9

SEND SECRET WISHES TO GOD...

If you find it hard to give voice to your innermost, secret longings, write them down in the silence of a quiet moment. Look at the words you have written. Transfer real and fervent energy into the words that describe your desires. Now close your eyes and believe that your wishes will come true. Keep these wishes inside a special 'messages to God' box and keep this box in the Northwest corner of your bedroom. You'll be surprised how fast God responds!

APRIL 10

YOU CAN DO IT, BUT ONLY IF YOU THINK YOU CAN...

When faced with an assignment that you feel is beyond the scope of the possible, invest some time in boosting your self-confidence. There is nothing you cannot do. When you believe in yourself something from inside you will respond and help you along. You can move mountains if you believe you can. So if you're given a tough project to prove yourself, don't get fazed. Just get started.

APRIL 11

THERE'S NO NEED TO BE A 'YES' PERSON ALL THE TIME...

How many times have you felt frustrated at being thought negative when you know how positive you really are? Being positive is today's magical buzzword but not everyone has the same definition of being positive. Is foolish optimism the same as being positive? And is falling in with every new proposal presented being positive? Don't be afraid to appear negative if that is how you feel! There is no need to be a 'yes' person all the time.

APRIL 12

YOU ARE NOT YET PERFECT...

If you are feeling inadequate today, for whatever reason, take heart. You are not perfect (yet). And neither is anyone else in this world. If we were perfect we would all be Buddhas. So don't give yourself a hard time each time you feel a crisis of confidence. You can only do the best you can and if that is not good enough for those who judge you – well tough!

APRIL 13

KEEP INITIAL GOALS EASY...

The secret to continuing success is simply to break down big goals into a series of little ones, and to start with the easy goals as you slowly make your way up the learning curve. This strategy makes achievement a lot easier and also a lot more fun! Success is much easier to accomplish when it is made up of a series of manageable steps. Occasionally you may get knocked a bit or you may have to take a detour. If you stay focused the ultimate goal will come within reach.

APRIL 14

THE POWER IS INSIDE YOU...

Today, you should listen to your soul. Tune in to the frequency of who you are. Listen with an accepting mind, and practise going deep within yourself. Create channels for the inner power to flow to the surface of your consciousness. Do not wait for another day. Today is a good day. Stop reading, pause awhile and then tune in to yourself by focusing inwards. Don't reach. Merely relax and keep the mind quiet. When thoughts intrude gently push them out. Practise this exercise often enough and one day you will connect with your inner power. When you do, you will exude a self-assurance that shows outwardly in a special kind of poise. Don't rush. Practice is the key to success.

APRIL 15

MAKE FRIENDS WITH THE CLEVER YOU...

Let thoughts flow smoothly and allow images to bloom inside your head. You may not know it but you have the ability to think through some pretty neat ways to reach your inner self and make each day happy and meaningful within your world. There is someone really clever within you. Inside your head are balms that can heal any hurt and medicine that can dress any wound. Inside you there is a storehouse of capabilities that can crystallise satisfaction at all three levels of existence, your mind, your body and your spirit. Don't stifle this impulse. Make friends with it instead.

APRIL 16

COMMUNICATING WITH THE COSMOS...

There is symbolic meaning in everything that materialises before you – be it a lame dog or an unexpected shower of rain. Accustom yourself to living in a state of awareness so that each new day finds you consciously conversing with the universe. With practice you will begin to understand the signs being sent your way. Develop the inner ear and the inner eye. Do not worry about how to do this. When you start tuning in to the vibrations around you, you will find yourself in complete harmony with them. Over time you will know the signals to heed and those to ignore.

APRIL 17

BE SINGLE MINDED WHEN RECEIVING SIGNALS...

Life's winners communicate positively with the cosmos, sending vibrant and positive messages outwards. They build on this communication and they watch their visions become reality. The cosmos always delivers. It fortifies any future you visualise for yourself. My advice to you is to tolerate neither distraction nor diversion despite setbacks and miscalculations. Be single minded when you look for signals. Be determined to put only the most positive interpretations on everything you see. You will not be disappointed.

APRIL 18

CELEBRATE THE WONDER OF YOU...

Some people are so good at envying other people that they miss out on what they are, what they have or who they can be. They simply cannot celebrate the wonder of themselves. Don't be like them. You are the child of an abundant cosmos. You can be everything you wish to be. You are exceptional and unique. Instead of envying others for what they are and what you are not, a state of mind that leads only to debilitating immobility or destructive jealousy, rejoice instead in what you are, in what you have and what you can be.

APRIL 19

EVEN A ROOSTER CAN TRANSFORM INTO A PHOENIX...

Even a humble carp can change into a dragon. Have you ever seen harmless animals transform into ferocious killers when circumstances force their backs to the wall, like a hen when her chicks are threatened? Overwhelmed by powerful maternal instincts even the lowly hen will find, from somewhere deep inside her, the courage to lash out at the predator threatening her brood. Somehow something triggers off determined, almost frenzied, clawing movements. It is the same with us humans. We possess enormous reserves of courage and can be quite fearless when sufficiently provoked. This only goes to show there is a passionate instinct within us that can take us to a different plane of consciousness where we can rise above anything that threatens us. Just think, if you could channel that same energy into overcoming your own unhappiness, how empowered you would be!

APRIL

20

A SWEET MOUTH CAN MOVE MOUNTAINS...

My grandmother used to tell me, 'Always start the morning with a bowl of sweetmeats. It will ensure your words stay sweet through the day, and a sweet mouth can move mountains.' And so it is. In the old days Ministers and concubines alike developed skills in verbal communication that could impart almost any kind of message – criticism, censure, praise or command – in the most exquisite language so that while the meaning was often clear, there was always a line or two of preamble that would ensure diplomacy. The correct choice of words can be exquisitely beautiful. Words can move the toughest general to tears and soften the hardest heart. Words can move mountains. Always choose your words well.

APRIL 21

MOONLIGHT CAN TURN EVEN DUST INTO GLITTERING JEWELS...

Nothing is quite as exquisite as the full moon on a cloudless night. Have you ever gazed at such a sight and watched as the moon's silver rays turn even dust into glittering jewels? The full moon is something magical. When you allow yourself to be mesmerised by the fullness of her glow, when she is at peak brightness, and you allow your thoughts to meditate on the range of emotions that she inspires, something stirs deep inside you. Unlike the sun's rays, which burn the earth, the moon soothes with her gentle radiance. The moon hides many secrets behind her beautiful façade. In the night skies, she passes from phases of pitch darkness to ultimate brilliance. The moon's presence in the night skies is cyclic – sometimes she is dark and other times she glows like a million jewels. Perhaps this is why it is so restful to take a meditative walk by moonlight. Who knows what moonbeams could open your eyes to?

APRIL 22

BE BOTH A WARRIOR AND A SCHOLAR...

Have you decided which you should be? Well, let me tell you, there is a time to be brave and a time to be smart. The warrior has the ability to endure the most severe physical hardships, and in the warrior's life there are countless opportunities to be brave, to be heroic, but also to be dead! The scholar is said to possess the fine mind; he is able to think and to strategise, but sometimes to such an extent that even as he plans someone sneaks in and kills him. Strive to possess the skills of both. Strive to be a smart warrior!

APRIL 23

THE SWORD AND THE PEN ...

Neither is superior. It depends on the circumstances of your situation. If you have a way with words do not think the sword cannot overcome you. And if you are a mighty fighter do not think you are immune to the man who is a skilful communicator. The real hero in life is the one who knows when to be a warrior and when to be a statesman, when to use muscle and when to use words.

A P R I L 24

AN INNER
CONSCIOUSNESS...

Rather than resist the confusion in your life, let your spirit guide
you. There is an instinct within you that will steer you safely back
to shore when you feel tossed on a stormy sea if you will only
develop a special channel of communication with it, and trust it.
This is the inner consciousness that has been with you all your life.
When you feel a need for a friend reach within for this inner guide.

APRIL 25

THE MAJESTY OF FLYING CRANES...

Flying seems effortless when you know how. Have you ever seen migrating cranes floating seemingly effortlessly in the sky, their movements executed in perfect symmetry and rhythm, their long, stilted legs flowing elegantly behind bodies that seem motionless? Their wings dance gracefully in rhythmic strokes up and down, moving forward through the stillness of the blue skies. Cranes move across the skies with such power, grace and majesty. We should move through life like cranes. We should live seemingly effortlessly.

APRIL 26

TURN ON ALL THE LIGHTS
IN YOUR HOME...

If you turn on all the lights in your house you will feel your spirits rise, especially if you have dark corners and there are insufficient windows to bring in outside light. This is a wonderfully easy yang-enhancing ritual which never fails to lift the lightness of chi. Lights have a special vibration which pierce the darkness of yin. Try this the next time you feel the air is heavy with a depressing energy.

APRIL 27

WEAR A FIRE RING...

Spend the day learning to make the most of elements that surround you. Take a leaf out of ancient Chinese wisdom and wear a fire ring to attract a busier social life. This attracts precious yang energy into your personal space. Fire rings are rings with precious stones that have glitter and deep fire hidden within them. Cut crystalline stones or cabochons with stars inside them can be described as fire rings. Naturally stones cut to a pyramidal point and that are red have the greatest amount of fire energy.

APRIL 28

FILL YOUR SPACE WITH SPECIAL SCENTS AND INCENSE...

Fragrant scents will make you feel good instantly. Different smells have the power to change the vibrations of your personal space. Make an effort to find out the incense that works for you, and stick with it. Natural scents work better than artificially produced chemicals. For me, personally, I have discovered the powerfully healing essence of plant smells, especially those derived from the leaves of plants grown in the pure air of high mountains. Mine come from the Solu Khumbu region of the Himalayas. It is called lawado incense.

APRIL 29

VERTICAL OBJECTS MAKE THE SPIRITS SOAR...

Did you know that vertical objects lift the spirits? So hang a long painting or invest in a grandfather clock. Vertical upward rising energy also brings wonderful growth chi into the home. It emanates a life force that is especially beneficial for homes with growing children. A great ritual to simulate rising energy is to light a single incense stick and then watch as the coil of smoke filled with incense slowly winds its way upwards and disperses into the invisibility of the room's chi.

APRIL **30**

MAKE AUSPICIOUS WORD AFFIRMATIONS FOR YOUR HOME...

Words that have strong positive connotations for you can prove an excellent means of starting to live in a state of enhanced motivation. The right affirmation could literally jump start you out of your lethargy. Often just the act of writing out strongly worded affirmations is enough to stimulate the mind into action and to get your subconscious mind working for you. Pin these phrases in places where they can send subliminal messages into your mind, like in your bedroom so that they are the first thing you read each morning when you wake up.

MAY |

WEAR YANG COLOURS IN WINTER AND YIN COLOURS IN SUMMER...

If you want to feel good about yourself try contrasting with the energies that change with the seasons. Since winters are yin, cold and often rather dreary, instead of wearing black, which seems to be so popular in winter, try wearing a yang colour. You'll be amazed what a difference wearing something red or yellow will make if you feel the need for warmth and a lift to your morale. And in the summer when your world is awash with plenty of bright yang energy, balance things out with some dark yin colours.

MAY 2

WEAR RED TO FEEL CHEERFUL AND BLACK TO FEEL ALLURING...

If you feel a need to cheer yourself up dig out some red clothes and let the colour work its special magic on your personal force field. And should you wish to feel seductive and alluring, simply sink into a little black number! Colours assert their own subtle influence over the way you present yourself to the world and this will transcend any initial impression. Colour will also provide the chrysalis for souls to connect for they have a truly profound effect on moods, emotions and responses.

M A Y 3

ABSORB THE YANG ENERGY
OF PUBLIC PLACES...

When you are feeling low or alone and wish to bathe your heart with happy yang energy, give yourself an hour or so in a public place where you know there will be lots of people. A yang energy bath is an excellent restorative for the person whose power levels have been depleted. You may have simply been tired out from too much work or because of stress. Lose yourself in a sea of people and let your spirit soak in the chi of activity. You should not go over the top on this, too much noisy chi is also not recommended. As always, balance is everything.

MAY 4

EMBRACE YOUR COMPUTER!

A revolution is taking place at your desk, the likes of which few have really yet come to terms with. We are on the edge of a totally new world, where the exchange of information, knowledge, and technology is being revved up to the speed of light. If you can wholeheartedly embrace the magic of computer technology today, it will definitely enhance your journey into the boundless. The new technology is moving alongside the renewed spiritual awareness of the world. There is a place in your soul for all that science brings into the equation of modern life.

MAY 5

GO SURFING...

The Internet is bringing the best the world has to offer into the privacy of your home and into your hands. Never before has the potential for such enormous amounts of information become available so easily and free of charge. Open your eyes to what is taking place in the cyber space around you. Even if you are an old soul you will benefit from the new discoveries. Do not dismiss these developments as being beyond your understanding. Take it from me. Often the only thing standing in the way between you and your computer is your own mental block. Transcend that and your world will have undergone a drastic transformation, especially if you have never used a computer before.

MAY 6

CHANGING THE ENERGY
AROUND THE WORK DESK...

If work at the office seems to have become a daily grind and you are feeling somehow dissatisfied with the way things are going for you, try changing the energies around your desk at work. Move your chair and table to a corner that is deemed auspicious. Follow element principles closely in terms of colour schemes and material energisers used and then enhance the chi of your desktop with other lucky symbols.

MAY 7

BE A PERSON OF ACTION...

Action oriented people make things happen. They do not just talk, or think or have endless rounds of repetitive meetings. Once an idea has been formulated and discussed and there is some kind of synergy and agreement, such people proceed with implementation without delay. People of action usually tend to really enjoy and master their jobs and are also usually the most upwardly mobile. You can be the same.

MAY 8

DON'T COMPLAIN AND NEVER EXPLAIN...

I learned two golden rules about making good conversation from someone rather wise. The first was to refrain from ever complaining about anything. There are simply too many people around with a righteous tale to tell. Complaining seldom makes anything better. It does not right a wrong and it rarely wins you friends. Always let fierce energy dissipate before engaging in conversation. The other thing is to stop explaining yourself. Explanations are nothing but rather long-winded self-serving excuses that no one really has any interest in or time for.

MAY 9

DON'T SIT OR STEP ON YOUR NAME...

Watch out for floor mats and cushions – the kind your favourite aunt lovingly embroiders for you. When you sit on your name or worse, when someone else sits on your name, you will be squashed, figuratively speaking! More harmful are the floor mats that are emblazoned with corporate logos and company names. Imagine the name of the hotel getting stepped on day after day by Joe public. It does no good for the hotel's reputation or business. So be sure that you are not letting your name get sat or stepped upon.

MAY 10

THE TIME TO BE STRONG IS WHEN YOU ARE FEELING DEFEATED...

If you have heard something negative said about yourself, something unpleasant, something unfair, something hurtful, something that causes you grief and worry, you could feel suddenly deflated and defeated. When you are criticised or become the victim of people ganging up on you, you may think this happens only to you. The truth of the matter is that this sort of thing happens to all of us at some time or other. In fact it happens all the time, everywhere, and no matter how weak you may feel then, you must take a deep breath and become strong. Never allow frivolous tittle-tattle to weaken you.

MAY 11

WHEN YOU HAVE A PROBLEM, DON'T SUDDENLY STOP THINKING!

It is really important to never allow problems to immobilise you. While there is nothing wrong in seeking support or guidance, you should learn to stand on your own two feet. Do your own thinking and turn inwards rather than outwards for strength and help. You must learn how to be mentally vigorous. Unless you make an effort to depend on yourself, you will find it hard to grow as a person. Start dealing with the small hiccups in your life. Before long you will have established a wonderful personal tradition – that of self-reliance.

MAY 12

DELIBERATELY AVOID CONFLICTS...

There is a lot to be said for taking the path of least resistance. Friendships are so much more satisfying when we actively adopt a strategy of non-confrontation. This is easy when you attach more importance to your friend's sensitivity than to your own. Watch your mind each time you see a conflict brewing, and then transform it by choosing the response that soothes rather than irks. Learn to give in, to compromise, or learn to walk away.

MAY 13

BE LESS JUDGEMENTAL...

As you get more advanced in age, your thoughts get more reflective and less prescriptive. Here is a clue to feeling good no matter what your age. You are never too young to become a philosopher. Just start to think in a detached fashion, engaging your mind rather than your emotions, and you will be well on your way to becoming non-judgemental in the way you interact with others.

MAY 14

HANG A METAL PAINTING...

Today, try hanging a metal painting in the corner of your living room, which is diagonally opposite the entrance. A metal painting is one that is made of metal, such as copper tooling. This will bring a wonderful benefactor into your life. It is really beneficial to have influential people in your life who can take on a mentoring role. If you want to enjoy this kind of luck try this easy energiser.

MAY 15

IT'S OK TO BE FRIENDS WITH FAIR-WEATHER FRIENDS...

Who knows how your friendship may develop, depending also on your own attitude. If you are honest with yourself, everyone is a fair-weather friend to some extent. Don't give up on someone just because he or she made friends with you to get something from you – that is, after all, what friends are for. Friends should be there for one another. If you have plenty to give at any time you should rejoice not only in your good fortune but also in your fair-weather friends. Who knows how you might inspire them with your generosity?

MAY 16

FLATTERY GETS YOU EVERYWHERE!

Indeed yes. It is so much nicer to spend time with someone who says nice things to you than with someone who is trying to make you into a 'better person'. There is an art to flattery. It really only works when you use it with sincerity. There's no need to be simpering or saccharine. Instead, just find something genuinely pleasant to say about the person you are interacting with. Making this small effort to look and comment is often the key that unlocks the door that leads to the secret corners of someone's heart.

MAY 17

WORK AT LOWERING YOUR VOICE ONE OCTAVE...

Try it. Pitch your voice a little lower. Instantly you sound better. When the voice is high it sounds screechy and unfriendly. It sounds hostile and even a little unbalanced! The most soothing tones come from people who have developed the art of pitching their voice at a pleasing level. A low voice is calming and wonderfully soothing. So work at lowering your voice one octave. You'll be surprised at how much nicer you sound!

MAY # 18

BUY A BRIGHTER SHADE OF RED FOR YOUR LIPS

Smiles look brighter, broader, wider and friendlier when lips exude happy yang chi. This only works for those of you whose face reflects too much yin. Bring colour to your face and watch it light up. A bright red lipstick is just one way. You might want to see what else could work for you. For me, I come alive each time I put on bright red lipstick!

MAY 19

SEND SOMEONE A FENG SHUI CARD ...

A feng shui card sends powerful wishes of good fortune, and the best intentions always succeed in brightening someone's day. Messages of love to people close to you should always be accompanied by the genuine wish for them to have the kind of luck they want or need at that moment of time in their lives.

MAY 20

SHARING YOUR SUCCESS IS A GREAT WAY TO SHARE...

Always acknowledge those who have helped you. Nothing makes anyone feel better than being genuinely recognised for the role they played in shaping your success. Sharing your success with them is an act of generosity and honesty that has the power to melt even the hardest of hearts!

MAY 21

SHARING THE MISFORTUNES OF OTHERS...

Even better than sharing your success with another, is to offer to share someone else's misfortune. When your friend needs a friend, let it be you. Don't wait to be asked. Frequently, all that is asked of you is your shoulder and a pair of non-judgemental, sympathetic ears to listen. But remember to really listen!

MAY 22

IF YOU WANT TO MAKE THE FIRST MOVE, DO IT!

Don't hesitate. So many people miss out on happiness because they hesitated and missed that moment when they could have reached out and told another person,

'Let's try being friends.'

Don't be shy. Shyness is nothing but a manifestation of the fear of being rejected. So let me tell you that there is nothing fearful about being rejected; it happens to the best of us and ultimately is of no consequence at all!

MAY 23

FRIENDS DON'T CHANGE ...

Only your attitudes to them do. When you feel that someone has changed towards you, the truth of the matter is that it is as much you who have altered towards them, your perception, your response, and your expectations, as they have changed towards you. You must accept that this change is inevitable. People move on and the rhythm of separate lives can cause the warmth of old friendships to grow lukewarm. Accept it.

MAY 24

WE ARE MIRRORS OF EACH OTHER...

How people respond to you is usually a reflection of how you respond to them. We are all mirrors of our own minds. We see what we expect to see, understand what we expect to understand. Our perceptions are coloured by our own experiences and by the benchmarks that define the parameters of our own worlds. That is why each of us sees the same person differently, why we have different opinions and different expectations. Accept this too.

MAY 25

LET THE WORDS OF GREAT MINDS INSPIRE YOU...

There have been so many great minds with so many gems of wisdom, and these have been put into words in exactly the way we need to hear them. Open your eyes and ears to the words of sages, poets, great men and women and let their words inspire and comfort you. Let their words strike a chord within you and then let them point the way. Spend this weekend at a library or in a bookstore looking for these words of wisdom.

MAY 26

FRIENDS SHOULD BE ENCOURAGING...

Wet blankets are like old raincoats; they should be put away in a storeroom and locked up, never to spread their dreary opinions or negativity ever again! If you are struggling to find the courage to pursue some course of action do not confide in anyone who is a wet blanket, no matter how young he or she is. Instead look for the soul who will share your dreams and who will rejoice in and accompany you on your journey of self-discovery.

MAY 27

IN PRAISE OF PRAISE...

Praise is a worthwhile habit to foster. Praise expands the inner spirit, builds confidence, makes the adrenalin flow and has the potential to create life-changing transformations in the person you praise. Be generous with your words of praise. After all, it costs you nothing!

MAY 28

DON'T BURST SOMEONE'S BUBBLE...

Ideas are wonderful inventions of the mind that go 'ping' in the head! Ideas are a very important part of someone's creative development. They are like vulnerable bubbles in the head, which can be expanded and built upon. They can be given space to float away, to fly, or they can be cruelly burst by some stupid, thoughtless remark. Be careful you don't burst someone's bubble!

MAY 29

THE SUBCONSCIOUS LISTENER IS MORE POWERFUL THAN THE CONSCIOUS LISTENER...

Be careful how you say things, how you phrase your opinions and your judgements. We all say things carelessly and lightly and then forget we ever said them, not realising they may have been picked up by someone's subconscious antennae. Injudicious remarks can later cause untold misery, unnecessary heartache or wilful misunderstanding.

MAY 30

COUNTER ANGER WITH OPPOSITE EMOTIONS...

The most pernicious of the three poisons that afflict the average mind is the poison of anger. It is anger that ruins all relationships that have previously been carefully nurtured. Anger is the one emotion, which has the potential to cause the greatest harm to your life. If you are feeling angry right now, know that anger can lead to misery, violence, and even death. You must deal with the anger inside you. Be ever mindful of anger rising and learn to counter any sign of it with opposite emotions, with love, compassion and understanding.

MAY 31

DON'T LOOK FOR MOTIVES
IN FRIENDSHIP...

The basis for befriending someone simply doesn't matter. You interact with people for all kinds of reasons and your motives are seldom so pure as to be above reproach. So don't penalise any friend of yours if you feel the motivation behind his or her friendship is to get something from you. And don't beat yourself up if you feel that you take them for granted. If you and your friend have something to offer each other you should rejoice. There is no nicer feeling than having something or being someone others have a need for. So rejoice!

Thinking About Friendships

JUNE

BE YOUR OWN BEST FRIEND!

Don't be your own worst enemy; don't sabotage yourself by putting the most negative and horrible connotations on everything you do. Instead, develop dedication to all the things that represent your world and yourself. Many things will happen in your life that will throw you off balance. So live your life to the full, giving yourself the fullest support and encouragement. Life cannot be part-time or half-hearted. You have to be ready to act on your own behalf all the time. This is what having deep-seated confidence is all about.

JUNE 2

FRIGHTENED PEOPLE ARE ALWAYS DEFENSIVE, SO SOOTHE THEM...

Be kind to those around you who may be intimidated by you. Sometimes without knowing it you may be sending out signals that keep people from seeing you as the ordinary, down-to-earth person you really are. You need to set the record straight, so you should make an extra effort to reach those who might fear you, rightly or wrongly. And if the fear is not directed at you but at something or someone else then you should lend them some of your courage, even when you are not feeling very courageous!

JUNE 3

THE DISCOURAGED ARE ALWAYS NERVOUS – BUILD THEM UP...

We all go through moments in our lives when we are ready to throw in the towel and surrender. At times like that what we wouldn't give to have someone strong building us up. How wonderful we would feel if we had the support of someone clever enough to remind us of our forgotten moments of glory. Compassion can be shown in many different ways but one of the most rewarding is to support and boost the confidence of someone feeling the weight of failure and rejection. Rejoice if you ever have the opportunity to do this for someone; you will find it very satisfying.

FORGIVENESS CREATES A POWERFUL SENSE OF LIBERATION...

There is something very damaging about holding a grudge. Nothing can be said for allowing hurt, betrayal and anger to fester in the heart. Like a raw wound, the pain just keeps getting worse and worse. On the other hand, when you let go of the root of the pain, there is a sudden yet real feeling of release. Forgiveness is the only thing needed to end wars. In the international arena this seems so hard to achieve but we can create peace in our individual worlds. Don't hold a grudge but forgive unconditionally and let peace enter your heart.

JUNE 5

ENHANCE YOUR
SOUTHWEST CORNER ...

The Southwest of any space, big or small, is where the chi of the maternal resides. The maternal is the nurturing earth mother, who yields rather than attacks. When you enhance this part of your living space with earth energy, with crystals or earthen materials such as porcelain, granite or stone you are engaging the nurturing spirit of 'yielding' and this attracts wonderful relationships into your life.

JUNE **6**

CRYSTALS CREATE GREAT FRIENDSHIP VIBES...

Crystals are the gems of the earth. They possess grounding energy but they are also powerful conduits for the inner flow of love that permeates the earth. Choose quartz and other transparent crystals for these seem to be the fastest catalysts for connecting with others and possess the greatest capacity for absorbing your own personal chi. Crystals placed in the Southwest are great for creating friendship vibrations around your space.

JUNE 7

FRIENDSHIPS LAST LONGEST WHEN THERE ARE NO EXPECTATIONS...

This is true of all relationships if you can live your life this way. It is hard not to expect commitment from someone close to you but if you are prepared to give up your expectations you simply remove the basis for anything to upset you. You will find that every wonderful act of love becomes a pleasant surprise that draws you closer in friendship. You will also discover that you can never be disappointed because you have relinquished your need to expect something in return.

JUNE 8

WIN AT CORPORATE POLITICS BY NOT DECLARING WAR...

I learned some valuable lessons during my years as a corporate high flyer. I discovered the best way to cope with corporate politics was to devise a winning strategy without declaring war. The secret is to practise a policy of non-reaction. Maintaining a sense of humour also helps since this takes the sting out of any 'poison arrow' sent your way, real or imagined, dissolving it before it hits you. Make an effort to ignore provocation at work. If you dismiss malicious gossip and treachery as trivialities, necessary nuisances too unimportant to waste time or sleep over, you deprive them of the energy to harm you. Then you will not declare war, and you'll win by default!

JUNE 9

SOMETIMES THE BEST STRATEGY IS SIMPLY TO WAIT...

When you are confronted with a decision that reflects ambivalence within, or a trade-off that you are reluctant to make, simply doing nothing is the best course of action. When I am uncertain about anything, or am unsure about how to proceed, I simply prevaricate and delay making a commitment. It is a good strategy to wait for the situation to unfold. This is not always the easiest thing to do. Patience is required. In the face of a crisis it is difficult to do nothing. Nevertheless take a lesson from the creatures of the animal world. See how so many of them incorporate waiting into their hunt and how this almost always pays off handsomely.

JUNE 10

THE WISDOM OF CORRECT TIMING...

There are days in summer when the scorching sun burns our feet and times in winter when icy cold winds freeze our fingers. Nature shows you how every environment changes with the seasons, with the passage of time. Likewise, for people, there is always an optimum time to do anything. Correct timing represents the greatest wisdom of all. When your timing is wrong even your best-laid plans will go awry and when your timing is right even mediocre arrangements will seem inspired. So if you want success, focus on the strategy of when to make your move!

JUNE 11

LEARNING LESSONS FROM THE BAMBOO...

The bamboo is regarded as one of the three friends in winter, the other two being the pine tree and the plum blossom. All three survive the harsh winter weather and even manage to thrive when the environment has turned unfriendly. When you find yourself going through hard times learn lessons from the bamboo. Learn to bend with the circumstances and blend with the conditions of the day. Bend as low as you have to. Only those who survive have the opportunity to bounce back when things improve.

JUNE 12

THE FIVE FINGERS OF MY HAND ...

The five fingers of my hand remind me of the five talents I need to develop and master in order to stay on top of any given situation: timing, skills, unity, prudence and courage. Timing requires patience. Skills call for dedicated study and practice. Prudence involves humility and thought. Unity requires harmony and sacrifice, and courage entails determination to overcome fear. This is the stuff of real wisdom!

Thinking Through The Strategy Of Life

JUNE 13

DILUTE BIG PROBLEMS INTO MANAGEABLE, BITE-SIZED MORSELS...

How easy it is to get overwhelmed by big problems. Try instead to chisel away at bite-sized portions of the problem than tackle the whole predicament all at once. Whether the problem is an event, an outcome, a development or a person, reducing it to bite-sized morsels allows the problem to become manageable. So it is too with strategies for success. Taken a step at a time, success will be assured. It is only the scope of the success that may be in doubt.

JUNE 14

INTERNAL DIAOLOGUES
WITH YOURSELF...

It is always a good idea to set aside some time to have a conversation with yourself. It is then that many deep insights into different issues surface. The mind has a way of storing within itself a wealth of buried wisdom. Make it a habit to talk to yourself. You never know what gems there are inside you until you make the effort to unearth them!

JUNE 15

LEARN FROM THE WINDS...

The winds change patterns and directions along with the seasons
and usually they change when you least expect them to. Difficulties
are the same. They occur and arise when we least expect them.
So anticipate the unexpected. Make this part of your plan for living
so that surprises no longer unbalance you.

JUNE 16

DON'T BE AFRAID TO BE A SHORT-TERM COWARD!

A judgement of courage or cowardice should depend on circumstances. There may come a time when you need to make a 'do or die' sort of decision, but remember it sometimes requires greater courage to retreat and withdraw, to take a couple of steps backwards. Don't be afraid to be a short-term coward. This could well help you to become a long-term hero!

JUNE **17**

MAJESTY BELONGS TO THE SURVIVOR...

There is no glory in death. Life is too precious. Majestic glory belongs to the one who is able to stand unperturbed in the midst of defeat and depression. Never give up on your life. Life is far too precious and there is no guarantee your next life will be in the human realm. So do not take your life for granted.

JUNE 18

WATCH OUT FOR THE TALL POPPY SYNDROME...

Be alert to the vulnerability of your own success. There is some danger in being noticed, in standing tall in a sea of mediocrity. The tortoise owes its survival to its unique ability to stay within its own protective shell. Stay low key. Do not be a tall poppy in a field of low poppies.

Thinking Through The Strategy Of Life

JUNE 19

NEVER GET CARRIED AWAY ...

Don't be lulled into a state of recklessness by the triumphant feelings engendered by small victories. Resist the temptation to surge unthinkingly into situations that hold greater risks than rewards. Preserve your strength. Bide your time. Stay cool. Go for the big victory!

GIVE UP A SERIES OF SMALL TRIUMPHS FOR ONE LARGE VICTORY...

Patience and self-control over the ego brings huge rewards. It's like winning the war rather than simply winning a series of small battles. Judge well when to lose some ground, when to make the sacrifices and when to move in for the triumphant victory.

JUNE 21

THERE IS MERIT IN DEVELOPING THE STRATEGIC MIND...

Strategy requires you to be mindful of your opponent's strength and alert to your own weakness. It is the inherently humble who ultimately achieve and deserve victory, for they never overestimate themselves nor underestimate the enemy.

JUNE 22

BENEFIT FROM EVERY KIND OF CHANGE...

When your attitude is one that embraces every kind of change, you do not waste time and energy wondering whether it is necessary. Instead you accept change as vital and you can then focus on dealing with it and coping with the new circumstances. If you are absorbed in the whys and wherefores and constantly seek out the person to blame for change, you will never get anywhere. If you react positively to a new environment you will benefit from every kind of change.

JUNE 23

TURN POTENTIAL
DISASTERS INTO VICTORY...

This requires a transformation of the mind, an attitudinal shift, which enables you to see events as having a deeper meaning, however negative or disastrous they may seem at the time. Do not view setbacks as final. See them instead as signposts that suggest a change of strategy or a different approach. Then your life and all of your life's pursuits will be ever meaningful.

JUNE 24

WHEN YOU'RE DOWN JUST PICK YOURSELF UP AGAIN...

Don't worry if you occasionally make a mistake, just get up and keep going. It is the person who keeps going that finally reaches the goal. Expect to make mistakes. It is the mistakes that will enable you to eventually tackle problems of greater severity. People who do not make mistakes will be like amateurs when confronted with the difficulties of later life.

JUNE 25

RESIST THE URGE TO BE IMPULSIVE...

Being impulsive is like water roaring down a waterfall, mindless, fast and racing downward, blind to the dangers below. When you act without thinking you are acting on impulse and you are out of control. It is far better to discipline yourself and let your opponents take that impulsive risk rather than you!

JUNE 26

BE MAJESTIC LIKE THE FOREST...

There is a certain inner power that comes from emulating the forest, which is deep, dark and filled with secrets, yet which stands majestically tall and seemingly unbending. Forests don't reveal their hidden strengths upon first sight and never their unknown weak spots. From the forest learn the importance of appearances, of hiding your secrets and staying majestically tight lipped!

JUNE 27

BE SWIFT LIKE THE WIND...

The wind manifests the dragon's breath, moving with a swiftness
that shifts the energy of the earth and sky. The wind refreshes the
energy of the land and, with the rains, shows the power of feng
shui at work. Be like the wind. Swiftly, surely, catch the currents of
contemporary thinking and move with them.

JUNE 28

BE FIRM LIKE THE MOUNTAIN...

Be strong and silent, resolved and calm, hiding your gold that lies within. When you stand firm like a mountain, all around you will take heart and be inspired by your show of strength and boldness, and all will be impressed by your stillness and silence. Keep your opinions to yourself and resist the urge to verbalise your opinion. The strong person is almost always a person of few words except when the occasion requires otherwise.

JUNE **29**

BE POWERFUL LIKE THE THUNDERBOLT...

There are times when it is necessary to be wrathful – but let your show of ferocity be like a bolt of lightning rather than a raging inferno. The bolt of lightning is blinding to the eyes. It is sudden and terrifying, striking with precision yet it lasts for only an instant.

JUNE 30

BE WELL RESTED, WELL FED AND WELL CLOTHED...

When your body is strong so too will be your mind. A hungry body houses a confused mind. A well-fed, well-rested body has a mind that is as sharp as a razor blade. Look after your body, tend it and clothe it well, and your mind, likewise, will stay healthy.

JULY

WHEN YOUR PATH IS BLOCKED SIMPLY MAKE A DETOUR...

This is such a simple truth yet so many people ignore this obvious solution. The best way to handle an obstacle is to go around it. There is no need to tear it down or fight it. Just move around it. It is the same with living. When confronted by someone obstructive just distance yourself and find another road.

JULY 2

MAKE EVERYONE LOOK GOOD ...

One of the best tactics in life is to genuinely strive to make everyone look good. This requires a secure mind and a generous heart. Make your colleagues shine and you will enjoy the luck of popularity. Make your boss look first-rate and you will enjoy the luck of upward mobility. Make everyone appear superior and you will simply look the best of all!

JULY 3

GENEROSITY GENERATES HUGE GOODWILL...

Nothing brings greater happiness than the practice of generosity.
Try it and see how much joy you get from the simple act of giving.
It is even better when you practise spontaneous generosity, such
as not even having to think when you give up your seat to
someone older than you.

JULY 4

DELETE THE WORD 'IMPOSSIBLE' FROM YOUR VOCABULARY...

Nothing is impossible. It is only your attitude, which makes you believe that something cannot be done or achieved. When you believe you can achieve a goal, you will. It really is that simple. You are what you believe. So today I want you to delete the word 'impossible' from your vocabulary.

JULY 5

SUCCESS COMES FROM GETTING STARTED...

Take a lesson from the famous Taoist teaching that the longest journey starts with the first step. Likewise the most arduous task also begins with the first step. There can be no success when your idea remains a thought. If you want to achieve something, anything, you must get started. You should not wait. You must steel yourself to take that first step. If there is something you really want to accomplish don't prevaricate, start!

JULY 6

ALLOW THAT YOU MAY BE WRONG SOMETIMES...

The biggest sin along the path to success is the sin of arrogance. The conviction that you can never be wrong is probably the most harmful attitude that works against you. The dogmatic, stubborn person is nothing more than someone who suffers from a hugely inflated ego. There are few vices more harmful than this. Don't let arrogance blind you!

JULY 7

CHANGE ANYTHING
EXCEPT YOUR VALUES...

It is fine to change course halfway. You are allowed to be fickle or to change your mind at any stage in your life. It is your values that should stay steadfast and sturdy, unwavering against the seas and tides of change. Values transcend space and time and give meaning to your existence. Shifting values suggest a life that has no solidity or purpose.

JULY 8

PROSPERITY PROGRAMMING VERSUS POVERTY PROGRAMMING...

Prosperity programming is the direct opposite of poverty programming. When you create limits in your life and think you're poor, you will become poor. The very fear of not having enough to last through your days will cause you to actualise a real lack in your life. So work at dissipating the fear of poverty, for it is this that will create obstacles to your becoming prosperous. Believe you will be rich and you will become rich!

JULY 9

PURPLE IN THE PROSPERITY CORNER...

Yes, try some feng shui! There are so many different ways of using feng shui to attract wealth luck. Placing a splash of purple in your prosperity corner is one way to do so. Your prosperity corner changes depending on the facing direction of your front door, according to flying star feng shui. For simplicity, the prosperity corner can also be the corner diagonally opposite the front door. Rest assured, there is nothing magical about this ancient practice but use feng shui only if you feel comfortable with it. Attracting wealth with feng shui is one of the easier things to actualise and the colour purple can help!

JULY 10

GIVING CREATES PROSPERITY VIBES...

Give freely and with no strings attached. Give with your heart and your head. Give with happiness imbuing your gift with strong happy chi. Always respond to someone who asks for help. Giving creates a vacuum, which attracts new wealth into your space. This sets up a flow that will constantly improve your lifestyle over the years. Once the flow gets going, it will not stop – unless you stop giving.

JULY **11**

SWEEP OUTWARDS WHEN YOU CLEAN...

When cleaning your home, always visualise getting rid of negativity and bad luck as you clean. As you visualise, sweep outwards. This gives the physical act of cleaning truly powerful energy.

JULY 12

FILL UP ALL THE EMPTY CONTAINERS IN YOUR HOME...

Unfilled containers suggest a lack, emptiness. So do fill any empty containers with things you want and love. Use children's toys if you want children, money if you want more income, sweets if you want sweet things!

JULY 13

USE BLACK AND WHITE COLOUR COMBINATIONS...

Using black and white is an effective way to jump-start a career that seems to be getting nowhere. This colour combination signifies the power of water getting stronger, and water translates into higher levels of chi in the workplace.

14

MAIN DOORS SHOULD NEVER BE BLOCKED...

When the entrance into your home gets blocked it closes off the source of new chi, which brings fresh opportunities to your family. Looking out of your front door there should be some empty space and looking in the same. This simulates the effect of the 'bright hall' inside and out and is most auspicious.

JULY 15

SPOIL YOURSELF WHEN YOU'RE FEELING POOR...

Go against the fear of adversity. Force yourself to do this. Unless you overcome your fear of adversity, you will never be able to make the quantum leap towards having and enjoying a state of abundance. So each time the fear grips you and you watch yourself turning miserly, go shopping and blow some money on something really expensive and probably frivolous that you've been wanting but have not dared buy.

JULY 16

MERELY LIKING TO BE RICH IS A MEDIOCRE FEELING!

You have to know about loving, about really wanting something without being obsessive. Merely liking anything is such a mediocre feeling it lacks the power to actualise your aspirations. You must want something wholeheartedly and you must believe you deserve what you want!

JULY 17

DARE TO FAIL AND YOU WILL SURELY SUCCEED!

The quality I truly admire in people is real courage. Not so much the courage associated with taking physical risks, although this too, but rather the courage that dares to risk failure. When you dare to look failure in the face, success is sure to come to you. This is because failure will never immobilise you. Failure will never cause you to avoid taking the kind of risks which bring spectacular success. Instead failure will galvanise you to try harder until the day arrives when success is yours!

JULY 18

LET EVERY BUSINESS FAILURE BE A LEARNING EXPERIENCE...

Every time you fall down on your face a valuable lesson is imprinted onto your mind teaching you what not to do wrong the next time. Experience becomes your ally. Experience is an expensive teacher because every business failure will cause you loss. But the lessons learned are invaluable. Learn even as you fail.

JULY 19

MAKE A 'WHY I WILL SUCCEED' LIST...

Make this list without worrying about the means you will use to achieve it. If you have to rack your brains and cannot come up with any convincing reasons as to why you should prosper, you are not yet ready for big success. On the other hand, if this list is too long, maybe you know too much and your self-assessment needs to be re-evaluated.

JULY 20

THINK IMAGES RATHER THAN WORDS...

The power of thought is infinite. But your attitude needs to be positive and you must be able to look beyond your immediate circumstances to the future that will take shape for you in the coming years. Think images rather than words! Unless you have these images clearly in your mind, your thinking will need some re-shaping. Thinking in images will richly encompass the vision and the dream.

JULY 21

SCARCITY THOUGHTS CREATE BLOCKS TO WEALTH LUCK!

Scarcity thinking means worrying each time you take out money to buy something to please yourself. Scarcity programming means being afraid to turn on the lights at night for too long, being sparing in the food you eat and frugal in the clothes you buy. If you are always worrying about the rainy day, soon my friend, you'll have a monsoon!

THINK OF THE UNIVERSE AS A TOTALLY ABUNDANT PLACE...

This is such a well publicised visualisation now that I am amazed how many still do not understand or appreciate the super abundance of our wonderful world. It is all in the mind. If you think of this universe as a place of plenty your base visualisation will set the stage for real abundance to come into your life.

JULY **23**

DECREE PROSPERITY FOR YOURSELF ...

If you decree prosperity for yourself it will materialise for you.
Everything in the world begins with the vision, the picture, and the
image. So when you can see all the pictures that accompany your
state of prosperity you will find yourself going out there and actually
creating it all!

JULY 24

ENERGISING WATER...

Here's some more feng shui. Try activating water to attract wealth luck into your space. For the Chinese, activating chi with water brings wonderful new prosperity but it should be placed correctly. Water placed wrongly causes money to flow outwards. Think carefully before you bring in the contractors to create your water feature!

JULY 25

FIVE RED BATS BRING GOOD FORTUNE...

If bats come and nest in your home, welcome them with open arms for they bring you luck! Other exotic 'pets' also bring wealth – the three legged toad, a pair of goldfish, the dragon fish, or the tortoise. Fake ones do just as well as the real thing.

DISPLAYING WEALTH SYMBOLS...

The Chinese firmly believe in creating cleverly worded statements to display in their homes. The most popular is the phrase 'Your Luck Has Arrived'. This is put on coins, auspicious paintings and all over Chinese decorative art. You can write this phrase in English and display it somewhere where you can see it on a daily basis. Before too long, luck really will come along!

JULY 27

HANG WEALTH ART ON YOUR WALLS...

Wealth art is well painted art which either contains auspicious objects or mountains of a certain shape and orientation. If the mountain is seen from the back, it should be turtle-shaped, if seen from the front it should be a wavy-ridged mountain. Alternatively, they can be pictures of special Taoist deities who are believed to bring good fortune vibes into the home. Remember that balance is vital and that you should never overdo any recommendation given in feng shui.

JULY 28

COMMUNICATE WITH THE COSMOS...

I am a great believer in listening to the signals sent by the invisible messengers of the cosmos. So I live in a state of awareness, ever alert to what the skies, the wind, the trees, the weather, my body, my dreams and even the events in my life are telling me. At first you will find it strange, this one-sided communication, but over time you will learn to sift the real from the mundane, the sublime from the ordinary. Listen with a keen ear and look at the world with watchful eyes.

Developing Awareness Of Space

JULY 29

FIND YOUR COMFORT ZONES...

Draw the line between belief and disbelief regarding everything you hear about the magic of undiscovered science. You don't have to accept as true everything you are told. Find your own level of conviction – and faith. Be relaxed in your investigation of the invisible energy forces of life. There is no need to challenge the unknown, but no need to embrace it immediately either.

Developing Awareness Of Space

JULY 30

DEVELOP AWARENESS TO SIGNALS...

When you read signs of good fortune or misfortune coming your way, your aura is heralding a time of expanded happenings, which may be good or bad. Respond to the happiness signals and push away the unhappy ones. You decide which vibration has the stronger influence in your life. Once you have chosen, happiness or unhappiness starts to unfurl.

JULY 31

ALWAYS LISTEN TO THE WARNING SIGNS...

Cosmic symbols that come your way do not always herald good tidings. Sometimes they are signs that warn of impending disaster. The signs are there for you to read and act upon. This requires awareness and sensitivity. Perhaps you start to lose things, or the car does not start, or you oversleep, or you forget where you've put your keys. Usually when more than three things seem out of sync, it is a good idea to pause and think and even to delay or cancel the meeting or trip you are just about to take.

A U G U S T

BEND LIKE THE WILLOW TREE ...

Sometimes the best route to take is to bend low in surrender. Losing does not have to mean the end. As long as you know when to acknowledge defeat, to bow gracefully and wait for happier times, the day will eventually come when you can prevail. Then you can enjoy your victory in splendour.

Developing Awareness Of Space

AUGUST 2

ORACLE DREAMING...

The Tibetans say that placing some kushi grass under your pillow when you sleep enhances your ability to recall prophetic dreams that waft through your sleeping consciousness. Kushi grass is the long dry grass that is often used to make brooms. The Chinese, on the other hand, say that merely by placing the statue or image of one of the Eight Taoist immortals behind your bed as you sleep, has the same effect. Keep a notebook by your bedside. If you do not record dreams immediately upon waking you will forget them by the time you are fully awake.

AUGUST 3

OPEN YOUR EARS TO THE SOUND OF WATER...

Softly trickling water awakens something magical in the environment. It sounds different to water that overflows, or falls from a height. Moisture in the air also brings its own special feelings of wellness and prosperity. When you live with the sound of water, nature blends in harmony with your soul. Your heart beats in time to the rhythms of flowing energy. It's a very good feeling!

AUGUST 4

WATCH A WATERFALL...

The rush of water transforms the atmosphere. Just think how powerful the fall of water must be to reach the bottom. No wonder it strikes the river below with such force. Just imagine the power of that downward momentum. Don't let your life go into free fall like the water. It is far better to flow along gently.

AUGUST 5

MOUNTAIN PEAKS JUST SEEM SO HIGH...

Mountain peaks appear to float in the sky and merge with the clouds. It is better to look down from a mountaintop than look up towards its intimidating peaks!

Developing Awareness Of Space

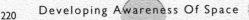

AUGUST **6**

IMAGINE IF YOU WERE A FARMER...

If you were a farmer, how sensitive you would be to the seasons, how close you would be to the land, how receptive you would be to the cycles of the Universe. For farmers, knowing the time, to the precise day, when the season begins to change is crucial and so it is with the cycles of life. Discerning when change is imminent enables you to experience oneness with nature, thereby making it easier to go with the flow. So develop the instincts of the farmer!

AUGUST

7

OBSERVING DOES NOT REQUIRE A REACTION...

The passive observer of life learns more from watching and viewing than from being an active participant. Refrain from compulsively intruding into other people's lives, with a need to voice your opinion. Outsiders rarely understand other people's circumstances so it is best not to interfere.

AUGUST 8

HOW LUCKY WE ARE TO BE A THINKING HUMAN...

The Buddhist texts reveal that the chances of being born a human are more remote than finding a turtle with a rubber ring around its neck in the middle of the ocean! Next time you feel depressed think about how precious your life as a human is, as opposed to being an animal, or a hungry ghost living in the demi-world between hell and human existence!

AUGUST 9

TAP MOON ENERGY TO
IMPROVE FAMILY LIFE...

On the night of a full moon, put out an urn of water so that it reflects the moon's light or expose a large single pointed crystal to it. Place the urn or crystal outside in the middle of your garden, or in a place where it can absorb the moon's powerful radiance. Then bring the water or the crystal inside to create wonderful vibrations that bring harmonious feelings of loving into your space. This feeling can last for the full cycle of the waning moon – about fourteen days.

AUGUST 10

BUILDINGS AROUND YOU HAVE ENERGY...

The buildings around your house radiate energy, very like a force field, that interacts with the energy of your home. Develop an understanding of these force fields so that you know if they bring you good or harmful chi. Usually, chi from buildings is good when bigger, taller and more imposing buildings are behind your home, lending support and protection, than in front of your house, blocking your luck and opportunities.

AUGUST 11

TREES BRING THE GROWTH CHI...

Old trees are like old souls – they are wise and benevolent. Tune in to them, particularly if they have been around for some time. Next time you go to the park pick out an old oak. Gently place your palms flat against its bark and your ear close to listen to the heartbeat of the tree. In a little while you will feel vital energy course through your veins as the tree responds. Taoist masters think nothing of using their palms to absorb some of this powerful growth energy of old trees. All you need is patience, strong concentration, pure motivation and a pair of sensitive palms.

AUGUST 12

ROCK FORMATIONS AROUND YOU HAVE MEANINGS...

One of the most interesting offshoots of landscape feng shui is to learn to 'see' animal forms and shapes in solitary rocks that dot the landscape. Old masters are especially good at detecting the silhouettes of frogs and tortoises, rats and serpents, dragons and tigers when viewing natural rock formations. And then, depending on whether the animal gleaned is fierce or benign and how the rock is placed relative to your home, they are said to bring abundance or disaster.

AUGUST 13

THREE PEAKS INDICATE SUCCESS FOR THE NEXT GENERATION...

There is an old belief that if you can clearly see three sharp peaks amongst the undulating hills in the distance, and these peaks are directly facing your main door, one of your sons will rise to great prominence amongst the ruling elite of your world and your good fortune will last through to the next generation. In other words all your children will enjoy happy and meaningful lives.

AUGUST 14

EARTH ENERGY BRIDGES HEAVEN AND MAN...

Taoist magicians believe that the energy of the earth is the chi, the dragon's cosmic breath, which can be searched out, discovered, and manipulated to ensure that it becomes an effective pathway through which heaven brings a flow of goodies to mankind below. This is feng shui – the clever harnessing of earth energy to actualise happiness for mankind. It's a technique worth learning!

SENSING UNIVERSAL VIBRATIONS NEEDS PRACTICE...

Don't lose heart if all this talk about energy and vibrations leaves you a little bewildered! To experience energy learn first to feel it within you. Stand with your feet slightly apart. Lift both arms and place them straight out, parallel to the ground. Now slowly bend your palms until they are ninety degrees to your arms. Hold this pose in a relaxed way and bring your attention to the palms of your hand. In less than a minute you should feel the energy slowly warming up the palms of your hands – this is chi, your inner life force.

AUGUST 16

SPEAK TO THE SPIRITS OF THE LAND...

Yes, there are land spirits! Make friends with the spirits who live with you in your garden and inside your home. These land spirits do not harm people unless they are disturbed. Speak to them and respect their space. There is nothing strange in acknowledging their existence. There are probably many different dimensions of life forms existing alongside ours. Do not fear them.

AUGUST 17

WHEN YOU FEEL TRAPPED BY CIRCUMSTANCES, USE YOUR MIND...

If you are caught in circumstances that make you feel trapped and you cannot easily break free, try to change your mental attitude and transform your problem into a source of joy. If you are the only person left to care for an aged parent, for instance, think how lucky you are to have this opportunity to create so much karmic merit or to repay a karmic debt. Your feelings are affected by the way you think. You can control the way you think, so think of your situation with gratitude.

Developing Awareness Of Space

AUGUST 18

THE EBB AND FLOW OF TIDES...

It is said that the moon influences your disposition. Your moods are affected by the pull of gravity, causing you to feel down and depressed according to how the tides ebb and flow. There is any number of valid reasons for your mood swings. But making the effort to resist the pull of gravity and to take back control of your moods is surely worthwhile!

WHEN YOU LOOK OUT OF YOUR WINDOW, LOOK FOR STARS...

Whether you find stars in your heavens depends on if you look up or down of course! This is the difference between those who are optimistic and those who are natural pessimists. The choice is yours of course but believe me when I tell you that optimists lead a happier, fuller and more satisfying life. So start to look for glittering stars on your horizon!

AUGUST 20

YOUR SPACE NEEDS CLEANSING REGULARLY...

Just as clothes require regular washing to feel comfortable, so do the spaces we occupy. Energy does get stale and stagnant, and it can get dirty and polluted so cleansing your space on a regular basis should be as natural as any other housekeeping ritual. Learning to purify your space will make your home a lot nicer to live in.

AUGUST 21

USING THE COSMIC ENERGY OF ELEMENTS...

You can use any of the five elements – fire, water, earth, wood or metal to cleanse your space. Fire energy takes the form of candle light and smoke; water takes its natural form; earth cleansing energy requires the use of salt; wood energy requires the use of special plants that create wonderful cleansing incense; and metal energy uses the sounds created by metal singing bowls and bells. It is particularly useful to learn some space clearing techniques.

Developing Awareness Of Space

AUGUST 22

METAL SOUNDS CAN CURE AFFLICTED ENERGY...

You do not need to know feng shui to use metal energy to cure your space of chi afflictions. Problems with chi can be created simply by the passage of time. There are complex formulas to understand how this works. But if you don't know this technique of feng shui you can still hang some metal wind chimes around the corners of your home and in rooms where occupants tend to get sick. Wind chimes will help reduce the effect of illness-causing feng shui afflictions. Metal energy is a very powerful feng shui antidote.

AUGUST 23

LOOK FOR THE MIRACLES
IN YOUR LIFE...

There are miracles happening every day of your life – if you only pause long enough to see and realise their occurrence. Anyone who waits consciously for miracles seldom sees them. The soul who understands the preciousness of life and human existence, who divines the quality of each new day, is the soul who is alive to the miracle of life itself.

AUGUST 24

HAVE FAITH IN YOUR OWN HUMAN CONDITION...

No matter what your circumstances or environment, no matter what your age or your place in the social fabric of your world, what is real is the faith you have in your own human condition. To recognise the miracles when they happen around you requires faith in yourself and this arises from a receptive attitude to changing circumstance and a wonder at the great unfolding Universe.

AUGUST 25

EACH OF US HAS OUR OWN SPIRITUALITY MAP...

Regardless of your starting point, or how you awakened to the spiritual dimension within you, once you have experienced it, no matter how briefly or in what circumstance, you will find it hard to let go. Even when you first ignore your spirit, it keeps nagging at you. Follow your own intuition, your own instinct. Pursue it. Different people follow different routes and it is perfectly fine to map out your own route, but never ignore your spiritual dimension.

AUGUST 26

AWAKENING TO YOUR REAL SELF...

There are so many ancient techniques to awaken to the real self these days; you are really spoilt for choice. The Hindu, Chinese, Tibetan and a host of other traditions seem to hold such enticing promises of wonderful worlds of great spiritual beauty and truth that it can bewilder your senses. Coming to terms with the many different lineages is not easy. In this then, let your inner self guide you. It has often been said that there are many pathways to heaven and no single tradition holds a monopoly on the truth. So follow the path you are most comfortable with.

AUGUST 27

MEDITATING ON THE CYCLES OF EXISTENCE...

I find I am mesmerised by the way Buddhist philosophy captivates all my senses, appealing on both gross and subtle dimensions – the logical, the spiritual, and the devotional – and engaging my heart, my mind, my body and my spirit. Meditating on the cycles of existence and being introduced to the concepts of karma (cause and effect) and samsara (the cycle of birth and rebirth) answered my questions about life and assuaged my confusion. Living the teachings of Buddha has been truly inspiring and has made me (I hope) into a better person.

AUGUST 28
KINDNESS AND COMPASSION ...

I am especially drawn to the central essence of the teaching of the Buddhist high lamas of Tibet because they instruct and live and breathe one major philosophy. They advocate kindness and compassion above everything else, calling this the development of the Bodhicitta mind and heart. Their consistency and sincerity is awesome. I bow low to their teachings.

AUGUST 29

AND SO THE GOOD IN ME BEGINS TO FLOWER...

When I listened to the words of my Buddhist high lama and applied his teachings to my everyday living, the good in me began to flower, and the bad began to fade. Like a lamp on a dark night he shows the way to the state of bliss we all call enlightenment. Let the good in you begin to flower too.

Mind Transformation

AUGUST 30

LOOK FIRST TO YOUR LOWER CHAKRAS...

We all have the Buddha nature – it just manifests at different times and in different ways. Other spiritual traditions also teach about love and kindness, the opening of the inner, good heart within us. If you are still rooted in the world of material pleasures alone and feel unready for spiritual growth, don't worry. It only reflects that your lower base chakras need satisfaction and appeasement before you can move to the upper chakras. Take your time. Just don't take too long!

Mind Transformation

AUGUST 31

LEARNING ABOUT THE LOTUS...

From muddy, dirty waters springs the magnificently pure lotus, beautiful, wholesome and untainted. Its radiance shines with the deepest of spiritual meanings. The lotus is the ultimate flower symbol of compassionate love. Even if your circumstances may at present be ugly and sordid, take heart from the lotus. Something pure and beautiful can still spring forth. Be comforted by this thought.

SEPTEMBER

ASTRAL TRAVELLING...

When I was very young – fifteen perhaps – I discovered Lobsang Rampa's books on astral travelling, and, while experimenting, I became aware of my astral body and the silver chord that joins it to my physical body. It was like discovering my higher self. Try lying down in a relaxed state of mind and feel yourself being gently dislodged from your physical body. Astral travelling is not for the faint hearted… so don't attempt this if you have a natural fear of the unknown. But allow yourself to go deep into another level of being if you want to know what lies there at the edge of our consciousness.

SEPTEMBER 2

A QUANTUM LEAP WITHIN OUR MIDST...

A quantum leap has happened within our midst – from physics to psychics – leading to a massive, explosive growth in all things metaphysical. As interest in esoteric mystical traditions grows, the mysterious holds us spellbound. We are living the quantum leap because it has now become mainstream to want to relate to who we are at all the three levels of consciousness – the body, mind and spirit. If you have already started along this exciting journey of discovery of inner consciousness keep going until you meet a perfectly qualified master who can guide you. When you are ready he or she will materialise.

SEPTEMBER 3

DO HAND MUDRAS AND FEEL THE TINGLE...

These are powerful hand postures and movements that are surprisingly graceful and extremely powerful. Performed accompanied by the chanting of mantras, hand mudras create wonderful magic and draw down upon us a mountain of blessings. Look closely at your fingers today and as you gently flex them feel them come alive with inner radiance... then feel the tingle!

SEPTEMBER 4

AWAKENING THE PSYCHIC INNER SELF...

It is said that everyone in the world has psychic abilities that they do not realise they possess. Psychic awareness need not be mysterious. It surfaces when you consciously start focusing attention on awakening it from within your inner consciousness. By doing this you are activating a hidden sixth sense which complements the conventional senses of taste, smell, touch, hearing and sight. The sixth sense is the powerful ability of insight – the ability to detect and tap into the senses in parallel dimensions.

SEPTEMBER 5

SAVOURING A STATE OF BLISS...

For a long time, I wondered why it was good to be moral, to live life in accordance with the ten virtuous actions, to be charitable, to help people, to be kind, to live a good life. If death wiped everything out anyway I thought there seemed equal reason to not live a good life as to live a good one. And then I was told about attaining the state of bliss, the sorrowless state, the state of no more learning, the state of permanent happiness that transcends space and time, that breaks free of life and death, birth and rebirth. This is the state of enlightenment, or Buddhahood. Now I know there is no higher goal than this state of bliss.

SEPTEMBER 6

ACTIVATING YOUR THIRD EYE...

Did you know that we all have an extra eye that lies just between our eyebrows on our forehead? This all-seeing third eye offers vision into the hidden depths of people's hearts and minds. I have been told that to activate the third eye requires years of focused concentration, bringing awareness to that part of the face and rubbing it with the right middle finger as you chant a particular Sanskrit mantra. I do this exercise for a few minutes each day and I chant the mantra of the compassionate Goddess Kuan Yin. You can use this mantra too, if you wish, it is 'Om mani peh me hone'.

SEPTEMBER 7

VISUALISING THE OPENING OF YOUR SEVEN EYES...

Later, as I delved deeper into the esoteric teachings of Tibetan Buddhism, I learned that we actually have the potential to open all the seven eyes of our physical body. The seven eyes are the three eyes on the face (two plus the third eye), two eyes on the insides of our palms, and two eyes on the soles of our feet. Activate these seven eyes by visualising them on your body as you meditate.

SEPTEMBER 8

A THOUSAND PATHWAYS TO HEAVEN...

Perhaps there are even more paths to heaven than we imagine. If we recall all the great spiritual teachers who have walked the face of the earth – Jesus Christ, Buddha Shakyamuni, Prophet Muhammad to name but three, they each showed a way, indeed many ways, to reach the ultimate in spiritual enlightenment. It is up to you to choose the way with which you have the greatest affinity and therefore the greatest chance of success.

SEPTEMBER **9**

SURRENDERING TO AN ENLIGHTENED SPIRITUAL MASTER...

There is something truly uplifting and safe about taking refuge under a spiritual master who is wise, kind and compassionate beyond anything you know. He or she encompasses what they describe as the triple gems of Buddha, Dharma (his teachings) and Sangha (the monks). The act of surrender signifies a complete renunciation of everything that hurts the world of living beings, the rejection of thoughts and deeds that cause suffering, and an embrace of all the good that lies within you. You should pray for a perfect teacher to come into your life who can inspire you to make such heartfelt promises of renunciation.

SEPTEMBER 10

DEVOTION BRINGS A MOUNTAIN OF BLESSINGS...

Blessings bring realisations of the highest wisdom, a knowledge that transcends space and time. True devotion generates a powerful love that surpasses the mundane understanding that comes only from ordinary learning. Devotion to a spiritual teacher creates its own momentum and enables you to mine real gold from within.

SEPTEMBER 11

HAVE YOU HEARD OF THE LAM RIM?

This is the graduated step-by-step path to enlightenment, the lamp that lights up the darkness of ignorance and guides the way to liberation. The lam rim forms the core of the Tibetan Buddhist path towards enlightenment – Buddha's secret teachings transmitted from one realised master to the next in an unbroken lineage that can be traced back to the Buddha himself. The lam rim puts liberation from the cycle of karmic rebirth into the palm of your hand.

THE UNION OF WISDOM AND COMPASSION...

Enlightenment is the simultaneous realisation of Compassion with Wisdom. Each by itself does not signify the divine attainment of the ultimate truth of existence that leads to permanent happiness. Compassion without wisdom lacks the understanding of the true nature of reality and wisdom without the genuinely kind heart is not wisdom at all.

SEPTEMBER 13

JUST A DROP IN THE VAST OCEAN...

Many of us think of our little worlds and believe we have seen it all. We think we understand everything, know everything. When in reality what we know, (and remember) is just a drop in the vast oceans of existence. The Universe is so vast! Think of yourself as just a tiny grain on the ocean bed and you will begin to realise the awesome expanse of existence. Or think of the scale of yourself in the context of the Milky Way! The feeling created is very humbling.

SEPTEMBER 14

IF ALL THIS SPIRITUAL STUFF IS TOO PROFOUND, GIVE IT A REST!

We are not enlightened beings. We are not Buddhas. We are not perfect and we cannot understand every nuance of every divine teaching immediately. All of Buddha's wisdom requires serious meditative thought. I try to share some of the words of my perfect teacher, especially those I judge the most important and beneficial, but I am not perfect. If I have trivialised the important, or stressed the unimportant, it reflects my imperfect mind. Those of you reading, whose knowledge is superior to mine, I beg you to judge these daily spiritual reflections with compassion.

SEPTEMBER 15

RAIN IS HEAVEN'S WATER...

Rain has such pristine qualities – it nourishes the land, cleans the air, and brings fresh new life to the ground. But rain can also be the devil's deluge bringing death and disease when it falls in torrents, blackening the land with blinding waves of water. Rain reflects the mind – it can be nurturing when it is beneficial but it can also turn wrathful when it is out of control.

LIFE IS A SACRED DANCE...

When movements are coordinated and sure there is so much grace and when there is also music life becomes a celebration! Performed under the stars and around the fire dances become ritual. Dance is elegant when it is measured, but it becomes frightening when frenzy sets in. So it is too with life. You decide if you want your life to be graceful or frantic!

SEPTEMBER 17

DO YOU NEED SUCCESS AT ANY COST?

Should the pursuit of fame and fortune become a death march through marshlands and jungles? Do you demand success at any price? Sometimes the cost of success is simply too dear, it can demand too great a sacrifice. Every now and then it is necessary to take stock of what your success is costing you. Remember that you do not need to pay any price demanded. If you're marching through marshlands you can choose to turn back, or to take a break!

SEPTEMBER 18

JUST LET GO...

When things get too much, just let go. Releasing is sometimes the best way to cope with life's pressures. You do not have to be strong all the time, determined all the time, empowered all the time. Don't let these 'achievement' gurus fool you. They too must have stopped many times along the way before they accomplished their own successes!

SEPTEMBER 19

FOUR TYPES OF PRAYERS...

You can be the judge as to which is the most powerful! First there is the prayer for wealth and success in this life. Second is the prayer for a good rebirth in the next life. Third is the prayer for total freedom from rebirth altogether, what they describe as liberation from samsara, and finally there is the prayer for enlightenment to benefit all other beings, the ultimate state of permanent happiness. Reflect on this and make your own judgement!

SEPTEMBER 20

BE NURTURING, LIKE MORNING SUNLIGHT ...

Precious yang energy, which has not yet become excessively strong, is the sunlight of new beginnings. Emerging from the dark night it is gentle and it soothes. It nurtures and does not hurt. This morning, give yourself a sunshine bath! Go into the garden to drink in the natural warmth of the Universe. Open your mind, your body and your spirit to the cleansing energy of the sun's light and even as your pores soak up the sunshine reflect on the nurturing quality of the sun. Think how it gives life and warmth to the earth, its plants and creatures each day, every day. The sun never fails. It is reliable and it appears every morning without fail. It is there even when we do not see it. Its presence is everywhere. Be like the sun in the lives of all your loved ones. Bring light and love and warmth each new day and feel how good it is to be nurturing like the sun.

S E P T E M B E R

21

NURTURE YOUR INTRINSIC SPIRITUAL ESSENCE...

Keep the mind blank and sit still like an un-carved block of stone. The best time to do this is in the very early hours of the morning. Sit while it is still dark, and as the sun starts to rise in the East feel the glow of the early morning sunrise. As the sun ascends, its rays give off a powerful energy – and soon it brightens the early morning sky. It is during these moments that your intrinsic spiritual essence will start to surface. Your good karma begins to ripen. When this happens, don't be deaf or dumb to the signs around you.

SEPTEMBER 22
A TOUCH OF MIST...

Mist makes any place entrancing. The sun's glow through mist transforms a simple mundane dwelling into the abode of some heavenly being. The picture that unfolds in your mind may take you to the pure land of the Gods – Shambala, Tushita, or the western paradise of the Buddhas, but what we think of as heaven exists within us. So tonight, close your eyes and dream of meeting the angels of Shangri la. Let a remembered existence from the past unfold within your mind. Do it gently. Don't reach.

Mind Transformation

ENJOY THE COOL AIR OF MOUNTAINS – GO FOR A SPIRITUAL RETREAT...

There is something truly magical about waking up very early in the morning and feeling the brisk cold air of the high mountains. There is nothing in the world like it. If you are the adventurous sort, go to Kathmandu in Nepal. Try to get a room in one of the monasteries that are nestled at the edge of the mighty Himalayas. I go to Kopan monastery each year, for teachings and a short meditation retreat. We wake up at dawn when the sun has not yet risen, and in the glow of twilight the clouds nudge at one's feet. I look out on a sea of clouds and it feels like I am walking in heaven. A little later when the sun rises I see mighty snow-capped mountains in the distance and it seems like I am floating through Pure land. These are moments of utter magnificence. It is a heaven on earth. Kopan is not hard to find. Just fly to Kathmandu. It nestles on a small hill just above the Boudhanath stupa. Ask for directions.

Mind Transformation

SEPTEMBER 24

A FALLING LEAF ON A WINDLESS DAY...

Think about negative karma ripening. We all have good and bad karma that has accumulated since the beginning of time. Karma follows us from one lifetime to the next and, unless purified, cleansed and dissolved, we cannot escape our negative karma. When bad things happen to us, such as when we fall ill, lose money, get cheated, or have an accident, it is the ripening of negative karma. Once ripened it gets wiped off our slate. So whenever something negative happens and we think of it as negative karma ripening, we should rejoice. Like a leaf falling down on a windless day, having fallen, it stays there.

SEPTEMBER 25
THE MANTRAS OF PURIFICATION...

The high lamas advise chanting karma-purifying mantras that cleanse all the negative karma accumulated over many lifetimes. This is the only way we can dissolve the blocks and hurdles that prevent us from making progress in spiritual advancement. The most powerful mantra of purification is Buddha Vajrasattva's hundred-syllable mantra but this has to be directly transmitted by a qualified high lama. What I can do is share the short version of this mantra with you. Say this mantra 28 times each day to get rid of the negative blocks in your life. The mantra is OM VAJRASATTVA HUM.

SEPTEMBER 26
SETTING UP AN ALTAR...

Place the image of a holy object of devotion onto an altar, where you can make daily offerings, real as well as emanated. A holy object can be a statue, a painting, a stupa or holy texts. It is excellent if a qualified holy master has properly consecrated the holy object. Daily offerings placed before the holy object can be bowls of water, flowers, incense, food, and candles. Supplement actual offerings with imagined ones in your mind. When set up with a pure motivation, an altar encourages awakening spiritual awareness, and creates the opportunity to bring a perfectly qualified teacher into your life. If you feel you are ready try it.

SEPTEMBER 27

THE SYMBOLISM OF HOLY OBJECTS...

When you make offerings to a holy object, you are not doing it to the statue or painting per se but to an abstraction that the statue or painting symbolises. You see, our minds are so deluded, so clouded and so impure that even if all around us there are a thousand Buddhas we cannot see them! Until our minds have become purified of negative karma, we can only see the statue or the painting. And so we imagine the Buddha in front of us, and we make offerings and prostrations as though the Buddha is in front of us. That is why we treat holy objects in such a reverential manner.

SEPTEMBER 28

IS RELIGION A LOGICAL OUTCOME OF THE SPIRITUAL PATH?

This is a useful reflection, which should be addressed by anyone keen on following the spiritual path. Surely spirituality does lead one to the deeper religious practices that require discipline and serious commitment. It is when we reach this stage in our personal journeys that focus and intense concentration require us to train our mind, our body and our spirit. Meditation does have a higher purpose, a higher goal than merely to reach within. We should always ask the question '…and then what?'

SEPTEMBER 29

DEVELOPING BODHICITTA – THE COMPASSIONATE HEART...

One of the highest purposes of meditation is to generate kindness and compassion towards all beings. Compassion is not merely feeling sorry for others. A whiff of superiority can taint this feeling. Compassion is not merely feeling pity either. That suggests the absence of the urge to do something about it. True compassion is generating the fierce desire to do something to alleviate the sufferings of others by oneself, alone if necessary, and to feel a sense of urgency about it.

OCTOBER

2

BATHE YOUR HOME WITH SUNLIGHT – BRING IN YANG ENERGY...

It is a good idea to give your home a sunshine bath at least once a day, if possible. In my country we get sunshine all year round so we never lack for yang energy. Indeed for us sometimes yang gets too bright and excessive so we introduce an occasional dose of yin energy to balance things out. The secret is to create a good balance of yin and yang.

W

Th

a

OCTOBER 3

CULIVATE INTERNAL STILLNESS OF MIND...

Mental calm will allow you to generate a sharp awareness of your surroundings. Quieting the mind is a prerequisite for beneficial meditation. The mind must be taught to discipline itself. Then, and only then, will you be able to push out mental sounds and chatter that distract and confuse. Practise stilling the mind with five minutes meditation once a day.

OCTOBER 4

THE PLUM BLOSSOM BLOOMS FROM SEEMINGLY DEAD STEMS...

The sight of the beautiful plum blossom inspires many Chinese poets and philosophers as it bursts forth from seemingly dead stems each winter. That such sweet beauty can emerge even in the midst of adversity must surely imply a deep inner strength. That is why the plum blossom is so highly prized as an auspicious symbol to have around the home during the New Year.

Revitalising Energy

OCTOBER 7

CLEAR YOUR KITCHEN CUPBOARDS...

People tend to forget to clean out the larder regularly. Food should never be stocked beyond its 'sell by' date. When food is allowed to get bad, stale energy instantly builds up causing illnes... chi to seep into the personal space. Make it a habit to clear o... kitchen cupboards.

OCTOBER 5

DO EVERYTHING YOU DO WITH GOOD MOTIVATION...

As long as your intentions are pure you have good motivation. Wholesome intention is the source of power that fuels all words and actions. Sometimes, however, even when the motivation is pure, the outcomes can suggest otherwise and then misunderstandings can happen. When such situations arise, remain calm. It is unnecessary to explain and best to say little. Have faith that eventually things will work out right.

OCTOBER 6

SWEEP OUT THE COBWEBS...

It is astonishing how quickly spiders build their cob... insects' corpses to be hung all round the home... amount of yin energy accumulating. Ugh! So s... cobwebs regularly. As you clean, think of th... blocks and hurdles of your daily life gettir... Incorporate this into your regular spac...

Revitalising Energy

OCTOBER 8

YANG ENERGY FOR HAPPINESS OCCASIONS...

Put some red in your life to create strong yang chi, especially during certain days of the year when it is so beneficial to wear red. The Chinese almanac recommends wearing this auspicious colour during 'happiness' occasions, such as wedding banquets, birthday celebrations for older people and month old celebrations to commemorate the birth of sons. Wearing red also makes you feel strong and ensures you don't get downtrodden.

Revitalising Energy

OCTOBER 9

USE WIND ENERGY TO BLOW THE NEGATIVES OUT OF YOUR SPACE...

This is a popular feng shui ritual that can blow away all the negative chi, which builds up over time. Make powerful affirmations that bless the home, protect the home and enhance the energy of the home and then write them onto cloth flags. String your banners up from tree to tree and let the wind blow through them. Each time the wind touches the flags your message is carried into the cosmos.

OCTOBER

LEARNING TO LET GO OF OLD STUFF...

Throw out broken belongings and feel the release. Chuck away television sets that do not work, computer terminals that have become redundant, broken doors, chipped teacups, clothes that no longer fit, umbrellas which are broken. It is hard to do and usually it is the sentimental soul who has the hardest time letting go. Yet attachment to things is such a negative habit. Unless you can let it go from your life you will forever be stuck in the past. So let go of anything you no longer need and move resolutely into the new millennium!

OCTOBER 15

BRING SPIRITUALITY INTO YOUR SPACE...

Use incense and holy aromas, nothing makes for better energy. Incense comes in many forms, as candles, aroma sticks, dried herbs and scented oils. When you use incense and fragrant herbs to lighten the energy of your space you are introducing a spiritual essence that transforms heavy, stale energy in your surroundings into sacred energy that is extremely light.

OCTOBER 16

ALWAYS CLEAR THE AIR AFTER A BIG FIGHT...

Even the most loving households have their share of disagreements and, over time, the afflicted energy of constant bickering causes the chi to thicken. Living in this environment is very unhealthy. Get a singing bell and use it regularly in all the corners of your rooms. The lingering, ringing sound will clear the air, making it light and crisp again.

OCTOBER 17

WHEN YOU'VE BEEN ILL...

Always cleanse the energy in your room after you've recovered from an ailment. Singing bells and bowls create the wonderful harmonics of metal. You can use them to purify the chi of a sickroom. When someone has just recovered after a long illness, you should also bring yang energy into the room by giving it a good airing and, if possible, a dose of bright sunshine to dissolve any lingering sickness chi.

OCTOBER 18
THE SOUND OF WIND CHIMES...

Wind chimes create powerful metal cures that overcome invisible killing energy. Of all the cures of negative feng shui caused by bad flying star energy, the most effective is the all-metal six-rod chime. The sound of softly tinkling metal slices through bad luck faster than the speed of light, often without you even being aware of it. Every household should have several wind chimes. Those with six hollow rods are powerful because the number 6 represents 'big metal'.

OCTOBER 19

BAD LUCK FROM THE EAST AND SOUTHEAST...

Bad luck emanating from the East or Southeast can be dissolved with a curved knife. Check the Chinese Almanac of auspicious days to find out the direction that bad luck comes from each day. If it originates in the East or Southeast, face those directions and gently cut the air three times with a curved knife.

BURN MISFORTUNES FROM THE WEST AND NORTHWEST...

When bad luck originates from the West or Northwest an easy way to dissolve it is to use nine lighted red candles. Candles create powerful fire element energy. Position the candles so that they face West or Northwest, depending on which direction the bad luck originates.

OCTOBER 21

SPRINKLE YANG WATER TO OVERCOME BAD LUCK FROM THE SOUTH...

When bad luck comes from the South you will need a large pail of water. To control bad luck from the South, gently sprinkle water in a southerly direction. Make sure the water has been energised in sunlight for at least three hours.

OCTOBER 22

DESTROY BAD LUCK FROM THE NORTH WITH TWO LUMPS OF EARTH...

Earth energy is excellent for overcoming the afflicted water energy of the North and if this is where bad luck is coming from on any given day, take two rocks or two lumps of earth and then sprinkle the earth in a northerly direction. Do this to dissolve bad luck if you have an important appointment or business transaction on that day.

OCTOBER 23

SUNBATHE YOUR PILLOWS...

All neck and shoulder pains disappear as if by magic when you give your pillows a good dose of sun! Do this on a very bright, hot day when the sun is almost scorching. Powerful healing heat from exposure to strong and direct sunlight can be absorbed and stored by your pillow.

OCTOBER 24

MEDITATE UPON YOUR NEEDS...

Examine your needs from every perspective. Look at your life from every angle. By the time you finish analysing and dissecting your needs, they will have modified and changed completely! They have succumbed to the power of meditation. When you see into the depths of yourself, it is easy to create a mindset that is in sync with the fulfilment of your needs.

OCTOBER 25
THE ULTIMATE RELEASE...

True release comes from knowing that death does not consume your soul, death is only the shedding of a skin. All the ancient civilisations of the world – Egypt, Tibet, China, and India – do not view death as final. The Book of the Dead imagines the soul passing on to another life. Reincarnation assumes different names and explanations, but all suggest a rebirth of the soul. It is to ensure the quality of the reborn life that makes what we do in this life so important, simply because the former depends on the latter.

OCTOBER 26

EVERYTHING IN BEAUTIFUL PERSPECTIVE...

As long as you have lived life with a good heart you will have accumulated much gold, much wealth, and many plus points in the realm of karma. Note that whilst upon death all material things disappear into nothingness, karmic gold translates into good human rebirth. Leading a virtuous life is like accumulating gold in your cosmic record book!

TAKE A NECTAR SHOWER...

The next time you sit down to meditate make a silent request to be blessed with a heavenly shower of nectar from the Goddesses of the Pure land. One of my favourite visualisations is to picture the Goddess of Mercy, Kuan Yin, standing on a lotus above my head. She holds in her right hand a small vial of pure nectar, from which she pours a stream of golden light into the psychic channels of my body. The nectar enters through my crown chakra and I feel totally invigorated. You can adapt this visualisation to suit yourself by using your favourite angel, god, goddess or Bodhisattva.

OCTOBER 28

MENTAL NITPICKING
CREATES MIND BLOCKS...

You may well find that bigotry and intolerance surface in you in certain circumstances. These preconceptions can block you from seeing the alternative standpoint, which could well be the powerful truths, which you are seeking to enrich your life. Don't allow prejudice, strong opinion, preconceived ideas and pride raise shutters in your mind. Each time you have a disagreement with someone which left you drained or angry, replay the repartee in your mind, taking the alternative stance. This exercise could well surprise you!

Enrich Your Life By Enriching Your Mind

OCTOBER 29
DO NOT BE AN
INTELLECTUAL COWARD...

Don't reject or dismiss ideas that come to you through mysterious or unconventional means. Do not fear knowledge that reaches you in an unorthodox way. In searching for new ways to enrich your life, it is necessary to let the mind wander along uncharted pathways. Wisdom seldom comes to those who are intellectual cowards. You must be brave!

OCTOBER 30

SEEDS AND SPARKS NEED TO BE NOURISHED...

There is a celestial spark and a magical seed within every individual. The spark can be fanned into a roaring fire, and the seed can be planted in fertile soil, and nurtured into a big tree. Do not be blind to all your wonderful potential, or you will forever miss the divine within you. Today, resolve to remove the eyeshades that have been preventing you from seeing what there is within you that can be nurtured, what within you that can grow and flourish!

Enrich Your Life By Enriching Your Mind

OCTOBER 31

SAVOUR THE SOUNDS OF SILENCE...

There must be good reasons why almost all the spiritual traditions of the world advocate some period of silence during the day when you stop speaking completely. In silence you will begin to hear others with an acuteness you never realised before. It is in silence that the mind hears all things loud and clear. Silence also trains your mind to be still and to be quiet so, in time, mindless chatter begins to fade. It is then that the inner you begins to rise to the surface.

NOVEMBER

THERE'S NO NEED TO UNDERSTAND EVERYONE...

There really is no need to understand everything or everyone in your life. Do not put so much pressure on yourself that you strain to understand things that perhaps it is better for you not to comprehend. This is also true of the people around you. It is not possible or necessary to know every little nuance of each friend and associate. Just accept people as they are at that moment in time. People reveal what they are prepared to of themselves!

Enrich Your Life By Enriching Your Mind

NOVEMBER 2

THERE'S NO NEED TO BE DEEP WITH EVERYONE...

It is also unnecessary to be everybody's best friend or attempt to become bosom pals with everyone you meet. There is much to be said about being superficial with people you have just met. By this I don't mean being fake or insincere, but allowing yourself to limit interactions to surface matters. There is time enough for exchanging confidences when the passage of time has allowed your energies to blend and harmonise and you discover yourselves to be kindred souls.

NOVEMBER 3

DON'T EXPECT OTHERS TO UNDERSTAND YOU...

When I was young it was as if I heard nothing else – the universal frustration of my peers complaining that no one REALLY understood them, not their parents, not their friends, not their loved ones. It seemed as if having others understand them became like a rallying cry for wanting to break free. Is there a need for you to be understood completely? Is this even possible? How can anyone truly understand you when maybe you don't even understand yourself?

Enrich Your Life By Enriching Your Mind

NOVEMBER 4

DIFFERENT PEOPLE PERCEIVE US DIFFERENTLY ...

This is because we put on different faces for different occasions. Sometimes you will forget this and wonder why office colleagues and neighbourhood friends seem to have such contrasting perceptions of you. You do not realise that you show dissimilar aspects of yourself to divergent audiences, at various times and during different stages of your life. The hybrids of persona within a single individual can be quite numerous. It is the same with your view of others. Your perception of a person may differ radically from someone else's.

NOVEMBER 5

WE SEE WHAT WE WANT TO SEE...

When we expect someone to be snobbish and judgemental he or she usually turns out that way, and yet when we watch the same person interact with someone else who expects to see only warmth and humility, the very same 'insufferable' person becomes someone else altogether – someone much nicer. So perhaps the people you dislike so much are merely reflecting back to you your own negative views of them! Try seeing positive qualities in people you dislike and watch them suddenly become rather agreeable.

NOVEMBER 6

LIFE'S BATTLES SHOULD LEAD TO GREATER HUMILITY...

When I look at my battle scars I remember the hardest moments in my life were those that forced me to confront my own weakness. Each of these hostile encounters were anything but civilised yet it is not the winning or losing that I remember. Rather, the cruelty of some of those encounters seemed to show me how little I knew and how afraid I could be. Over the years the intensity of conflict gave depth to my appreciation of humility and wisdom. I discovered the release of surrender. With this it seemed as if the struggles became less dramatic and far easier to deal with.

NOVEMBER 7

DISCIPLINED THINKING MUST SPRING FROM HIGHER GOOD...

Disciplined thinking opens many doorways into the vast storehouse of wealth that lies dormant and hidden within you, but it should not arise from blind adherence to rules. Instead, discipline should spring from the will to attain a higher good. There is something divine in the disciplined mind but you should develop this for the right reasons. Your goal should be to benefit as many people as possible.

NOVEMBER 8

YOU SHOULD NEVER GO BACK ON YOUR WORD...

People are attracted to honourable friends like bees to a honey pot. The most important facet of honour is the genuine endeavour to keep promises. The Chinese take this very seriously. For them, a handshake is often good enough when it comes to giving one's word. To renege on even a verbal pledge means a loss of face too severe to contemplate.

NOVEMBER 9

DON'T BE AFRAID TO CHANGE YOUR MIND...

Sometimes it is necessary to depart from what has previously been arranged. When circumstances dictate a volte-face or a withdrawal of your support, even if the consequences of your change of plans may be far-reaching, don't be afraid to change your mind. However, you must also be ready to face the consequences of your actions!

NOVEMBER 10

DID YOU KNOW THAT THE BAMBOO IS HOLLOW INSIDE?

I have had wonderful moments of meditation contemplating the void that runs through the length of the bamboo stem. It makes me realise the significance of the void. I contemplate what is not there rather than what is, in what is not said rather than what is said. At meetings, so often what is left unspoken is of greater significance than what is voiced. Another interesting point about the bamboo is that it is the hollow in the centre of the bamboo that gives it its remarkable ability to bend without breaking. Take a lesson from the bamboo and meditate on the void within you – this is the first step towards grasping the true nature of reality.

NOVEMBER

SUDDENLY YOUR LIFE MAY CHANGE...

Not enough people think seriously about the inconstancy of life. They assume that things will never change, that circumstances will always stay as they are, until something tragic happens. Few of us anticipate our partner walking out on us, or being told we no longer have a job or losing a loved one forever and then it is too late. Picking ourselves up again will be that much harder for in our complacency we grow an attachment that sets the stage for intense suffering. It can lead to immobility when our lives get ripped apart. Contemplate your life and the nature of Nature itself.

Enrich Your Life By Enriching Your Mind

NOVEMBER 12

WHAT IS A DOOR TO YOU?

A door is heavy, thick and immovable. Do you see doors as obstacles? Do you think of doors shutting in your face? Or do you think of open doors that are entrances through which you walk into new worlds and new experiences. If you think of doorways as entrances rather than as obstacles, yours will be an attitude that has access to a great many wonderful experiences. What you need to do then is to find the keys that unlock the most important doors in your life!

NOVEMBER 13

THE FINAL STROKE...

I am told that the old style kung fu masters who created lethal fighting sequences rarely imparted the most destructive final stroke in the sequence. They withheld their secret even from their most trusted disciple. As a result their powerful undisclosed movements died with them. Why did these kung fu masters guard their secret to their grave? It is very likely that they could not bring themselves to reveal the way to ultimately defeating them. When the final stroke is known, a counter move can be created. By withholding the final stroke the element of surprise is always theirs in case they have to fight for their own survival. Take a lesson from these old masters. Share the critical element of your particular skill – which is like gold – only with those most worthy of your trust.

NOVEMBER 14

NEVER TAKE GOOD FORTUNE FOR GRANTED...

Last night I had a chat with my daughter, Jennifer. I had just moved her to another room in the house to enjoy better feng shui for the next few months. I asked her if she felt any difference after moving. She said that it did not seem like her life had got any better. So I asked her if she could think of any really bad thing that had befallen her and she shook her head. However, she did acknowledge that her life seemed smoother, with none of the minor accidents and bad luck of the early months of the year. It is funny how when we don't have serious bad luck we just takes things for granted. Why does bad luck have to strike before people appreciate their good fortune?

MAKING YOUR HEART YOUR CONSCIOUS ALLY ...

The Chinese believe that the heart represents the core of our mental continuum. Focus on the heart as the essence of your whole being, and after a few moments of silent communication, listen to the responses from your heart on all choices facing you that you are unsure about. Sometimes the heart sends a physical response and you feel a sudden sensation in some part of your body. At other times the answer comes in a sudden 'ping' of realisation. A person, object or event flits suddenly into your mind to set you thinking. With practice you can open channels of communication with your heart until they become totally natural for you. Before long your heart becomes your ally, helping you to develop a spontaneous intuition.

NOVEMBER 16

BASIC ELEMENTS
TRANSCEND ALL OF LIFE...

The complex nature of all things can usually be broken down into basic elements. Understanding this helps us appreciate them better. For example, foods basically comprise five main tastes – sweet, sour, spicy, bitter and salty which, when blended, become a meal. Plants, despite their variety, comprise roots, stems, leaves, flowers, and seeds. All music comes from a few basic notes and all the colours of the world are an amalgamation of primary colours. Most things comprise basic elements which when studied separately make them easier to grasp. So too with life. Look at the basic elements of your life if you want to analyse what makes yours real for you.

NOVEMBER 17

RISING TO THE
OCCASION...

We do not know how we will rise to the occasion until that occasion comes. Would we surrender and give in or put up a fight when confronted with danger? Would we lead when all hell has broken loose? Would we be able to cope with a major setback requiring instant action? Rising to the occasion depends on the moment itself. Never try to predict your responses during times of crisis. We do not know how we will respond and react. When occasions like this arise, steady yourself and stay calm. Take a deep breath. Do not allow yourself to panic. If courage is needed, be brave. If help is required, go out and search for it. Dissect the task facing you into manageable-sized pieces and then proceed to tackle them one at a time. If you keep busy you will not have time to doubt yourself.

NOVEMBER 18

WHEN YOU DOUBT YOURSELF, COURAGE FLIES OUT OF THE WINDOW...

If you are wondering whether you can cope with whatever is bothering or facing you, and you feel afraid, this is when underlying doubts about your ability and your staying power will begin to set in. When this happens, fight the misgivings. When you question yourself fear wells up and courage flies out of the window. Everyone is afraid when they feel unsure or incapable. This is a natural feeling. It is the one who acknowledges and then conquers the fear who will have the guts to keep going. And those who conquer fear are the ones who embrace the potential for true greatness.

NOVEMBER 19

ONCE SPOKEN, WORDS CAN NEVER BE RETRACTED...

It is so important to be skilful with words, and to learn to hold your tongue when you are flushed with anger. Words are like a double-edged sword. Smooth words of flattery can ease tension but words can also carry the heat of fire and have the power to inflame passions. Once spoken, they can never be retracted. The wise man holds his words in check when he has nothing useful to say or when what he has to say will create bad blood and ill feelings. Learn to hold your tongue – it is a wonderful habit to cultivate.

Enrich Your Life By Enriching Your Mind

NOVEMBER 20

WATCH FACIAL EXPRESSIONS...

Sometimes facial expressions do not tally with sweet words of flattery. If you want to charm someone, or impress someone or merely wish to get on the right side of someone, be sincere and genuine when you use words of flattery to get yourself noticed. There is nothing more annoying than facial expressions that belie words of praise. What comes across is really unattractive as it implies your listener cannot differentiate between fake flattery and genuine praise.

NOVEMBER 21

BE SUBTLE – NO ONE LIKES AN OBVIOUS PERSON...

When you master the fine art of understatement you will realise that subtlety is more powerful than brute strength! Being subtle means being mysterious, means saying less rather than more, and having perfect mastery over oneself. There is never a need to show off or take the credit for anything. You go through life confident enough never to state the obvious or to draw attention to your own cleverness. Subtlety is the hallmark of the real master. The bonus is that many people find it irresistible!

Enrich Your Life By Enriching Your Mind

NOVEMBER 22

'VIRTUES OF HYPOCRISY' SHOULD BE REJECTED...

One of the things I most disliked about my days as a corporate high flyer was how I had to develop what I used to describe as the virtues of hypocrisy – mouthing niceties I did not believe in, saying the opposite of what I meant, feigning honesty while I told half truths, and generally making small talk through endless cocktail and dinner parties which I pretended to enjoy. If I had not got out in time I fear I might have capitulated. That is the norm in corporate behaviour so if you are as allergic to all of this as I was; you might want to have second thoughts about your desire to move really high up the career ladder!

NOVEMBER 23

BEING CREATIVE IS A DIVINE FEELING ...

Think of the painter who is able to capture the depth of feelings inspired by beauty – the gentle clouds that nudge at your senses, birds flying majestically in the skies, the rippling flow of streams or the blossoming of a flower. Being able to express your thoughts, opinions, happiness and sadness in a powerfully creative way must be a divine feeling. So nurture your creativity no matter what else you do in your life. Don't miss out. Follow every opportunity that allows you to express yourself and watch as your creativity transforms you into a deeper, more fully aware, child of the Universe.

NOVEMBER 24

INTERNAL CONVERSATIONS
REVEAL DEEP INSIGHTS...

I always find time to talk to myself. It is when I retreat into myself to engage in serious self-debates and dialogues that flashes of insight and occasional moments of brilliance rise up to the surface. Internal conversations reveal a wealth of buried wisdom. These internal dialogues offer wonderful solutions to niggling problems and stunning new ideas that take me from one level of attainment to another. Let your conversations with yourself be serious and profound. Engage yourself in self-debate that addresses issues you do not understand, on subjects that require clarification.

NOVEMBER 25

LOOK AT THE ASSUMPTIONS BEHIND ANY PROPOSAL...

When offered a scheme or proposition it is always a good idea to look immediately at the conjecture that lies behind the idea proposed. The pillars that hold up almost any proposal are the theories upon which it is built. Assumptions can be reasonable or ridiculous. By focusing on them the soundness of the ideas themselves immediately becomes obvious.

Enrich Your Life By Enriching Your Mind

NOVEMBER 26

MEMORIES CAN LIE BURIED...

Painful memories of past mistakes, defeats and failures are usually buried deep inside the conscious mind. Over time these layers of memory get buried deeper as fresh memories are laid on top. This is the defensive mechanism that enables us to reduce the agony of past mistakes. But it also means hard lessons do not get learned. When the mind buries the deepest, darkest failures or mistakes, it is like sweeping things under the carpet. So the lessons of the past stay forever buried. Have the courage to shake loose your painful memories. You will become stronger when you confront them. They will also lose their power to hurt you.

NOVEMBER 27

IN RELATIONSHIPS DON'T LET WATER FREEZE INTO ICE...

When hostile differences between you and another are allowed to ferment for too long, a serious conflict between you could become inevitable. When that happens, no one wins. So if there is someone who inflames and infuriates you, make an effort to cool the anger within. Take a conciliatory approach – as much for the other party as for you. It takes a bigger person to issue the white flag. In so doing you will ensure that water does not harden into ice.

NOVEMBER 28
EVERY BETRAYAL IS A KARMIC EPISODE...

Karma is the law of cause and effect. When we describe events as karmic episodes we mean that at some time in one's past either in the present life or in lives past, the cause was created for the event to happen. So if you have just been the victim of a betrayal this means that you created the cause for this to happen, perhaps in some past life. Your attitude should thus be to rejoice that you have finally settled a karmic debt. Looked at this way the betrayal instantly loses its power to hurt. More, it creates greater mindfulness of the way you interact with people and hopefully it might even make you feel a twinge of regret.

NOVEMBER 29

KARMA IS CAUSE AND EFFECT...

It is as much within your power to create the causes for your future happiness, as it is to create the cause for your future unhappiness. You are the one responsible for creating the positive and negative events in your life, both the one you are currently living and future lives! The choice is yours. The more good you do to others, the more good will be done to you. As you sow so shall you reap. We are presently in the period of the kaliyuga when the ripening of good and bad karma happens really swiftly, so what you do in this life will ripen in this life! Remember, you can be a conscious creator of happy events!

NOVEMBER 30

DETACHMENT IS THE POWER BEHIND THE FULFILMENT OF DESIRE...

The potential of the human mind to actualise outcomes is enormous. However, the first tenet to practise is the detachment that accompanies desire. When your desire for anything is accompanied by a strong attachment to its outcome, the chances are that the power of your desire is considerably weakened. For the power to be real and to lead to fulfilment, always practise complete detachment, and then your dearest, deepest wishes will come true.

DECEMBER 1

BE SERENE WHEN FOCUSING ON THE THINGS YOU WANT...

It is when you succeed in being relaxed and calm that your practice of mind actualisation becomes really powerful. You will succeed in holding a fixed focus so that your mind becomes laser sharp in intensity. The result is a magical serenity that will allow you to succeed in attaining potent, detached awareness. At this stage you can turn your attention to any goal, object or outcome and it carries with it a most powerful focus, the kind that creates the reality. This succeeds because detachment implies the most powerful belief in oneself. Practise single-pointed meditation to achieve intensity of thought, and observe detachment to give it real power.

DECEMBER 2

USING MIND POWER REQUIRES YOU TO LET GO...

If you plan to use the power of your mind to actualise visualised desires, do not worry about how they will come about. Let the cosmic power inside you take care of the details. If you start worrying about how you can achieve all you have asked for you will only sabotage the cosmic plan meant for you. Never forget that the scope of fulfilment could be so grand as to be outside your own limited vision. Just let go, and let the cosmos surprise you!

DECEMBER 3

SECURITY IS AN ILLUSION...

Security represents nothing more than a strong complacency to the circumstances of your world. Real security does not exist. It is merely a label your mind invents to fool you into fearing the unknown. There is no growth and no freedom in hanging on only to what you know already. On the other hand, if you are able to shake off this attachment to the familiar, and can embrace the uncertainty of all your tomorrows, you would have taken a quantum leap in opening fresh doorways and original manifestations. Life will suddenly take on new dimensions for you.

DECEMBER

DON'T LET LONG-TERM
PLANS BE RIGID...

I prefer living from day to day. I have always kept diaries to record my thoughts as I live each day rather than to pen in dates and fixtures for the coming weeks and months. I don't really need to know what I will be doing or where I will be next week, or next month. My dates and plans keep changing and all the most wonderful experiences of my life happen at a moment's notice anyway! Allow for unexpected opportunities to come along. Don't hesitate to rearrange your calendar to accommodate them. Being rigid could allow you to miss out on significant events that might change your life forever.

ALLOW SOLUTIONS TO EMERGE OUT OF CHAOS...

Have faith in the fabric of your existence. When you face some hard choices and are at a loss to what to do, you should never feel compelled to seek desperate solutions. Instead just do nothing. The more harassed you are, the more hopeless you feel, the more you should shrug your shoulders and symbolically let the burden slip off your back. Develop real indifference to any outcome to your problem or situation. Briefly think through what is the worst that can happen and then shrug it off. Then watch as the situation begins to right itself. You will discover that out of confusion can often emerge something quite fabulous that is of real benefit to you.

DECEMBER 6

PROBLEMS OPEN UP NEW OPPORTUNITIES...

Each time you are confronted with a problem that brings you face to face with uncertainty, note that it can be beneficial. Uncertainty can bring you fresh new opportunities, whether you can spot these openings or even acknowledge them as such depends on your attitude and your state of awareness. If your eyes are always alert to all the things the Universe sends your way, you will not miss any of the opportunities presented to you.

DECEMBER

DISCOVERING THE TRUTH ABOUT YOURSELF...

By now you know already that the true self is totally spiritual. You know that all of us here on Earth are spiritual beings manifesting in physical bodies. When we die we are shedding one skin and preparing for another. So in order to enjoy your life to the fullest you must discover your spiritual self. Only then will the divine in you surface and the golden light within start to shine forth. In discovering the truth about yourself you will awaken to the true nature of reality and the real purpose of your existence. It is only then that you achieve the permanent happiness that comes with the ultimate realisation.

DECEMBER 8

DISCOVERING YOUR PURPOSE IN LIFE...

Spiritual awakening creates clarity of awareness about your real purpose in this life. When you realise how everyone seems to have a 'gift' – the ability to do something so much better than others – you begin to accept that we are all here on this earth for a purpose. The sooner you discover what your purpose is, the sooner you can begin to make your life meaningful.

DECEMBER 9

STRIVING TO FIND YOUR VOCATION...

This means you should strive to find out what it is you do really well, and what it is that makes you really happy. Nothing brings greater fulfilment than to be doing what you truly love to do. When you find out what moves and inspires you, have the courage to break loose of any chains that may be binding you and do what you need to do with a confident heart and mind.

Enrich Your Life By Enriching Your Mind

DECEMBER 10

DO NOT WORRY ABOUT MUNDANE TRIVIALITIES...

When the time comes for you to break free of your present life, just do it. There are moments in your life when it is simply essential to follow your heart, especially when it comes to creating a life and lifestyle that will bring you closer to your spiritual self. Don't worry about mundane trivialities like survival or the future. Have faith that the Universe will provide and that you are living a cosmic plan. In the 1980s, when I discovered I had had enough of being a banker, I simply resigned and did something else even though at that time this meant giving up one of the most prestigious and powerful jobs in Hong Kong. I decided that my karma as a banker had finished and it was time to move on.

DECEMBER 11

BEING OF SERVICE TO OTHERS...

The realisation that one can actually feel great joy being of service to others is divine. This is not a feeling or conviction that comes to just anyone. You need to have good karma to feel like this. Think about the people in your lives. How many of them do you know who actually enjoy helping others? How many would feel such an attitude to be foolish and a waste of time? And how many would ask 'What's in it for me?' if you asked them for help?

DECEMBER 12

THE ULTIMATE REALISATION...

On the other hand, if you feel that helping others is the real purpose of your life, this indicates that you possess the ultimate realisation that leads to unlimited spiritual growth. Make a strong and heartfelt commitment that the purpose of your life will be to dedicate yourself to being of service to others. From then on watch your spiritual awareness begin to unfold, develop and flourish.

DECEMBER 13

THE SELF-CHERISHING MIND...

All our suffering, without exception, derives from the wish to please only ourselves. This is the self-cherishing mind in action, the mind that has no thought to benefit others. It is said that when we are able to break free of this mind, which focuses exclusively on the self, then, and only then, can we realise our own delusion. So while we go in search of our spiritual self, our higher self let this not be a search that revolves around the self-centred 'I'. Because this 'I' is only the ego, not the true spiritual self.

DECEMBER 14

THE ROOT OF FEAR IS ATTACHMENT TO THE SELF-CENTERED SELF...

If you wish to have complete control over fear then you must understand that the fear you feel is proportionate to the amount of concern you have for your egotistical self. When you transfer that concern from yourself to someone else, fear instantly vanishes. Consider this, if only you are in danger you feel very afraid but if you and your child are in danger, you transfer your focus to your child and are concerned exclusively to ensure his or her safety. So when you are concerned about someone other than yourself there is no fear, just devotion to another's welfare. All fear comes from attachment to the self-centred self.

DECEMBER 15

THE WISH-FULFILLING GEMS...

When I first studied under my lama he urged me to seek out people who annoyed me and to look on them as wish-fulfilling gems. 'Use them to practise patience!' he urged. Friends who support you and who say nice things to you always make you feel good so you have no chance to practise. Strangers, too, are not very helpful because they will be polite to you. But people you find annoying will always try your patience, thereby giving you a chance to practise the art of patience. Treat people who irritate you as wish-fulfilling gems, for they are your teachers!

DECEMBER 16

DISPELLING ANGER...

Anger is one of the three poisons of life. So many of us are born into this world with a great deal of suppressed anger and we make so little effort to control it. And yet anger is such a terrible affliction because it has the power to destroy relationships which have been built up over the years. We should make a concerted effort to overcome anger. Once again, you should seek out people who make you angry and practise the antidote to anger – patience. If you find people to practise on often enough, a great deal of the anger will dissipate.

A SPIRITUAL ANTIDOTE TO CONTROLLING ANGER...

I was told that a powerful anti-anger purification ritual was the simple act of making daily water bowl offerings to holy objects like a statue or painting of Buddha, or to a consecrated stupa. To do this practice you will need an altar and seven medium-sized water bowls made of metal, porcelain or crystal. If you can, it is a good idea to add a tiny bit of saffron to the water to symbolise the creation of nectar.

DECEMBER 18

MAKING WATER BOWL OFFERINGS...

Each morning make fresh water bowl offerings to Buddha. Wipe the bowls clean and then cleanse them further with incense smoke. Fill the water bowls with yellow saffron water. Fill them to the brim, without spilling any water, and as you fill silently say the words, OM AH HUM. Then carefully arrange the water bowls next to each other in a straight line. The bowls should be close but not touching – one rice grain width between them. In the evening, pour the water into a container and use the offering water to make tea. Clean the bowls and turn the empty bowls over so the altar does not look empty. Repeat the offering ritual the next morning. This practice will make it increasingly easier for you to control your anger. Performing this ritual every day is a powerful karmic purification practice.

DECEMBER 19

A DEPTHLESS OCEAN OF SUFFERING...

If this is how you are feeling at the moment – perhaps your wife or husband has just walked out on you leaving you disoriented and unbelieving, or you have lost a dearly beloved to an illness or an accident and you are unbalanced with grief – consider that life or samsara is the nature of suffering. Samsara is one of the four noble truths. The cycle of life always ends in suffering – we grow old and we die or we lose our loved ones. Everyone experiences suffering at some point in his or her life. The only way to deal with grief like this is to accept that this is the nature of samsaric existence, and then to develop a strong wish to be liberated from this continuous cycle of suffering – let your loss open up the spiritual path for you.

DECEMBER 20
HARDER THAN DIAMONDS...

Everything comes from the mind. Yet, unlike your body, you cannot see the mind because it is colourless, shapeless and formless. Ignorance, anger and attachment are all products of the mind, and like the mind, are invisible, yet they can be harder than diamonds, harder than the Rocky Mountains. So the mind is all-powerful. It creates the world and it engenders happiness and suffering. The key to happiness is therefore the ability to subdue and control the mind.

DECEMBER 21

HAPPINESS AND SUFFERING COME FROM THE MIND...

Since happiness and suffering come from one's own mind, rather than from an external source, it is necessary to eliminate thoughts that bring suffering, and to cultivate thoughts which bring happiness. Thoughts that bring suffering are negative thoughts, the wrong philosophy, and the wrong attitude. Following the right teachings, teachings that bring joy and happiness to you and those around you, engenders positive thoughts. By studying, listening, reflecting, and practising positive meditation, you will eventually succeed in subduing the negative mind and happiness will be your province.

Enrich Your Life By Enriching Your Mind

DECEMBER 22

JUDGE ALL ACTIONS BY THE MOTIVATION BEHIND THEM...

Here's a tale that explains motivation. The story goes that someone passing a statue of Buddha in the rain quickly put shoes on the head of the statue to protect it. Shortly after it stopped raining somebody else came by and said, 'Oh, how terribly disrespectful – someone has put shoes on the statue!' and took them off. Motivation is the essential standard by which to judge the virtue of actions. Both people created the opportunity to be born as 'wheel-turning kings' because both actions were done with good motivation. The motivation at the precise moment of the act is especially important in deciding whether the act should be considered virtuous or otherwise.

DECEMBER 23

EACH TIME YOU DO SOMETHING GOOD, DEDICATE IT...

There is karmic merit in doing good, in helping others and in practising the kind heart. So each time you do something good dedicate it immediately to someone or some outcome you are praying for, otherwise all the merit attained simply goes to waste. Karmic merit gets wiped out instantly when you become angry or perform some non-virtuous action like lying or cheating. Dedications are prayers. Amongst your dedications should be the fervent wish to develop the genuinely kind heart.

DECEMBER 24

A POWERFUL DEDICATION...

One of the most powerful dedications, which I use daily, is the wish that the 'good heart' will arise strongly within me. The phrasing I use is this; 'By the positive merit created by this good deed, may the good heart in me not yet born arise and grow, may that born have no decline but increase forever more.' In Sanskrit the good heart is called Bodhicitta. So dedicate your good deeds to the development of Bodhicitta.

DON'T BE IMPRESSED BY 'MAGIC' ...

Magic is but a word to describe a phenomenon we don't yet understand. Often magic is just an illusion that fools one of your senses. But there is also the magic of clairvoyance and of precious jewellery materialising in front of your eyes out of thin air. When you see people walk over fire or water, read minds or make their heartbeats slow down you marvel. These and many other phenomena are yogic acts that demonstrate a kind of superhuman ability and are performed by those who have mastered very advanced control over their minds. But a word of warning, don't be impressed by these feats to the extent that you lose yourself entirely to them!

DECEMBER 26

FORMIDABLE MASTERS OF THE MIND...

Acts of magic, such as expanding a supply of food or mind-reading, reflect the abilities of holy men called yogics who are formidable Masters of the Mind. To know the truly enlightened Master however, you should also realise that such men almost never make anything of their powers. Genuine masters are extremely humble, often to the extent that you overlook them, so it requires a special awareness to notice and find them. Do not mistake magic performed by someone using the ordinary powers of passing land spirits as the real thing!

DECEMBER 27

MATERIAL WEALTH – HOW MUCH IS ENOUGH?

I have a great deal of patience for young people who are hungry for success and for material wealth. They are still working on satisfying their lower chakras, and it is understandable if they have not yet reached the stage of saying they have enough. But if you are a mature person, who has lived life, you know that your needs and tastes are easier to satisfy as you get older. You have little left to prove and your ego requires less flattery. Your spiritual needs also become more important. How much you need before you have enough depends on what stage of life you have reached.

DECEMBER 28

INNER POWER COMES FROM RESPECTING REAL TRUTH...

You have almost a year of reaching within yourself behind you. Now is a good time to take stock. Ask yourself if you have been completely truthful with yourself. Have all the issues you meditated and reflected upon been free of distortions and error? Do you feel you have attained some level of progress and do you understand the Universe better? Can you work effectively with energy and can you tune into the balance of chi within yourself and the space around you? Inner power comes only from respecting the whole truth and the real truth.

LIFE ISN'T ABOUT
WINNING OR LOSING ...

Now you know that life is about realising your potential so that you can be of maximum benefit to the greatest number of people. Life signifies actions that make your existence really meaningful. Then you can become a fulfilled individual, enjoying a most special kind of happiness. How fully you can achieve this state depends on your past karma, and also on the combination of your heaven luck, mankind luck and earth luck.

Enrich Your Life By Enriching Your Mind

THE LONGEST JOURNEY BEGINS WITH THE FIRST STEP...

Whatever you decide to do with your life, to change and transform your life, once you have decided, begin. The hardest task starts with the first move. The longest journey begins with the first step. With that vital first step you are on your way!

DECEMBER 31

AND SHOULD YOU OCCASIONALLY STUMBLE...

If you fall, simply pick yourself up again and keep going. The secret of a happy life is never to stay down for too long. Always get up and travel on. Move along with the flow of time. Today is the last day of this year ... tomorrow is a brand new year. Try standing extra tall tonight as you flow along with the passage of time. Programme yourself to prepare for an even better year than the one just past. Open your heart and your mind and let the New Year fill you to bursting with brand new energy!

Enrich Your Life By Enriching Your Mind

GLOSSARY:

Bodhicitta: A Sanskrit word which means the compassionate heart, having an altruistic intention.

Bodhisattva: An enlightened person who has reached enlightenment through the attainment of realisations of the ultimate reality – wisdom and compassion – thereby reaching Buddhahood but who has not yet become a Buddha because he/she wants to show others how to reach it.

Bright Hall: A phrase used in feng shui to describe an open area in front of a house or inside the front door which is considered most auspicious since it allows benevolent chi to accumulate before entering through the door into the home.

Chi: The life force or vital energy of the Universe. It is most auspicious when it is benevolent and meandering and is most inauspicious and killing when it moves excessively fast and straight.

Dharma: The ideal truth as set out in the teachings of Buddha.

Living in Dharma means living a life of morality with the motivation of attaining enlightenment for the sake of all beings.

Dragon's Cosmic Breath: The lyrical phrase used in feng shui to describe benevolent chi or auspicious energy.

Ego: The self-cherishing mind.

Feng Shui: Literally translated as 'wind-water,' this is the Chinese system of balancing the energy patterns of the physical environment in order to attract good fortune and avoid misfortunes.

Guru: A wise leader who leads one to freedom from worldly cycles of birth and rebirth (known as samsara) and to the attainment of enlightenment.

Kaliyuga: In Hindu mythology, the current age of the world.

Karma: In Hinduism and Buddhism the law of cause and effect. The concept of karma states that all actions lead to positive or negative karma which follows us like a shadow throughout our life and into future lives and existences. As we move from one rebirth to the next, good karma creates good rebirth circumstances while bad karma results in bad rebirth circumstances.

Kuan Yin: The Chinese goddess of Mercy – a Bodhisattva who answers all prayers.

Lam Rim: The step-by-step path to enlightenment in the Buddhist tradition.

Lama: The spiritual guru who leads one towards enlightenment in the Mahayana form of Buddhism practised mainly in Tibet and

Mongolia.

Poison Arrow: A feng shui term used to describe any sharp, pointed or straight structure from which negative energy emanates, bringing with it ill fortune.

Samsara: The endless cycle of birth, death, and rebirth.

Sangha: Buddhist monks and nuns and the spiritual community.

Sanskrit: An ancient language from India, the language of the Vedas and also the language of the Buddha.

Shambala: The name of one of the Buddhist Pure lands.

Stupa: Traditionally the place where the Buddha's holy relics and ashes are kept. Today a stupa is a holy object said to symbolise the Buddha's holy body.

Tushita: The name of another Buddhist Pure land. Tushita is the pure land of the future Buddha Maitreya.

Yang: The intrinsic nature of life energy, life, brightness, daylight, the sun. Yang is one of the complementary opposites in Chinese philosophy, reflecting the more active, creative, warmer aspects, but it cannot exist without Yin.

Yin: The diametrical opposite of Yang energy, death, silence, darkness, the moon. Yin is co-dependent on Yang for existence. One of the complementary opposites in Chinese philosophy, Yin reflects the more passive, still, reflective and receptive aspects.

Yogi: A person who is a master of spiritual yoga – the highest form of yoga.